POSTETHNIC AMERICA

Also by David Hollinger

The American Intellectual Tradition: A Sourcebook
Co-Edited with Charles Capper

*Science, Jews, and Secular Culture: Studies in
Mid-Twentieth Century American Intellectual History*

*In the American Province: Studies in the History and
Historiography of Ideas*

Morris R. Cohen and the Scientific Ideal

POSTETHNIC AMERICA

BEYOND MULTICULTURALISM

David A. Hollinger

TENTH ANNIVERSARY EDITION WITH
A NEW POSTSCRIPT BY THE AUTHOR

BASIC
BOOKS

A Member of the Perseus Books Group

Designed by Ellen Levine

Library of Congress Cataloging-in-Publication Data
Hollinger, David A.
    Postethnic America: beyond multiculturalism / David A. Hollinger.
        p. cm.
    Includes bibliographical references and index.
    ISBN 0-465-05992-9 (paper)
    2005 Edition:
    ISBN 10: 0-465-03065-3; ISBN 13: 978-0-465-03065-1
    1. Pluralism (Social sciences)—United States. 2. Multicultur-alism—United States. 3. United States—Race relations. 4. United States—Ethnic relations.
I. Title.
E184.A1H64 1995
305.8'00973—dc20
94—40366

06 07 08 / 15 14 13 12 11 10 9

To my Berkeley colleagues

CONTENTS

PREFACE

Visiting New York City for the first time in 1967, I was astonished to see at the corner of Seventy-second Street and Broadway a group of Amish men. The long beards, wide-brimmed hats, and plain black coats identified them for me as some kind of Pennsylvania Dutch. They reminded me of photographs of my grandfather. In an instant I realized that they could not actually be Amish. Neither the hats nor the coats were quite right, and I could not imagine the stay-at-home Amish making even a brief visit to Manhattan. Clearly, they were members of some other group. So, I said to my fiancée, a native New Yorker, "Look at those Mennonites, or they may be Old Order Dunkers." She smiled patiently and said, "No, those are Hasidic Jews." Then she added, "My roots, not yours."

If yet another lesson were needed in how little one

learns about people from appearances and in how greatly appearances themselves depend upon the beholder's eye, here it was. The plain attire had served my imagination the way skin color and facial shape often serve to make Koreans and Japanese look alike. The cultural differences between a family of fifth-generation Boston Unitarians and a family of fifth-generation Texas Baptists will be missed if we see only that both families are black. Or white. Bodily shapes and colors are not so easily changed as suits of clothing, but they are often taken as indicators of a person's culture.

The multiculturalism of our own time has helped us to recognize and appreciate cultural diversity, but I believe this movement has too often left the impression that culture follows the lines of shape and color. There is no doubt that racist understandings of what shape and color mean have limited the kinds of cultural choices and creativity people can achieve. But *Postethnic America* is written in the belief that Americans need to push yet harder against the authority that shape and color have historically been allowed by society to exert over culture.

This essay on cultural diversity in the United States grows directly out of my experience as a historian specializing in the history of American academic and literary intellectuals. Among my long-term interests has been the transformation of American intellectual life by the ethnic and religious diversification of its demographic base. In the late 1980s and early 1990s I began to supplement these historical interests with more contemporary engagements. At a series of conferences and campus workshops, I tried to contribute historical perspectives on the multiculturalist debates and found myself increasingly caught up in these debates themselves.

I want to acknowledge the criticism and encouragement of a number of colleagues and friends, especially within the remarkable faculty of the University of California at Berkeley. I cannot list here the names of all the people I have in mind when dedicating this book to my Berkeley colleagues. This large company includes many people not involved in the particular project of writing this book. I cannot even mention all those from whom I have learned something important about the issues addressed in the book. Yet I do want to thank Thomas W. Laqueur, Thomas C. Leonard, Robert C. Post, and Yuri Slezkine for detailed and extremely valuable advice. I am also grateful for the collegial stimulation on diversity issues provided by Todd Gitlin, Jon Gjerde, Martin Jay, Peter Sahlins, Jeremy Waldron, and Reginald Zelnik. I owe a special debt to Carol J. Clover, who, more than any other single person, persuaded me that what I had to say about multiculturalism must be in the form of a book rather than merely articles in scattered journals.

Beyond Berkeley, I have profited greatly from the critical suggestions of Thomas Bender, Charles Capper, Kenneth Cmiel, Judith DeWoskin, Kenneth DeWoskin, Don

Herzog, Daniel J. Singal, and Ronald G. Walters. At Basic Books, I have been blessed to have so able an editor as Steve Fraser. Paul Davies and Charles Raymond Katz have performed a variety of library-related tasks with an efficiency and goodwill for which I am grateful. My greatest debts, intellectually and personally, are to my wife, Joan Heifetz Hollinger.

Some sections of this book are taken from three articles previously published: "Postethnic America," *Contention* 2 (1992); "How Wide the Circle of the We? American Intellectuals and the Problem of the Ethnos Since World War II," *American Historical Review* 98 (1993); and "Cultural Pluralism and Multiculturalism," *Blackwell's Companion to American Thought* (1995).

November 1994

*   *   *

How can a democratic society achieve political cohesion while recognizing cultural diversity? The inability of most immigrant-receiving western European nations to come up with good answers to this question has become increasingly apparent during the ten years since I first published this book. As European societies struggle with the diversity presented by their Muslim populations, the perspective on culture and politics outlined in *Postethnic America* seems to me all the more pertinent to global as well as to America-centered discussions. Hence I am grateful to Lara Heimert of Basic Books for inviting and overseeing the publication of this new, tenth anniversary edition, which includes a new chapter, "Postscript 2005: Ethnoracial Mixing and Economic Segregation." The text is otherwise exactly as it was when first published 1995 and as supplemented by "Postscript 2000" in the second edition.

Berkeley, California
August 2005

POSTETHNIC AMERICA

CHAPTER I

Introduction

Multiculturalism is a prodigious movement, but its limitations are increasingly apparent. It has not provided an orientation toward cultural diversity strong enough to process the current conflicts and convergences that make the problem of boundaries more acute than ever. Mixed-race Americans demand recognition from the United States census, while many black politicians defend a "one-drop rule" for identifying African Americans that was designed to serve slaveholders and white supremacists. Women's rights activists try to help victims of clitoridectomy, while cultural relativists warn that westerners have no standing to instruct Saudis and Sudanese on culturally specific rights and duties. Educational reformers add new cultures to school curricula, while guardians of civility demand the banning from campuses of speech that might offend certain groups.

Illegal immigrants from Mexico complicate the public services of California, while prophets of "postnationality" explain that the boundary between the United States and Mexico is an imperialist fiction.

That multiculturalism is not more helpful in interpreting these boundary disputes derives, in part, from its prodigious character. Multiculturalism grew rapidly in the 1980s and early 1990s by directing itself in simple terms against an evil widely resented, the narrowness of the prevailing culture of the United States. It drew energies from a multitude of constituencies and was invoked to answer an increasingly wide range of questions. But its unifying principles have proved too vague to enable its adherents to sort out their own agreements and disagreements, and its vocabulary is not precise enough to parse the very different problems to which its followers look to it for help. Multiculturalism is like many historic movements that speak compellingly to the anxieties and aspirations of a distinctive historical moment, but are then inhibited from meeting new challenges by the generality of the commitments to which they owe their existence: it has outgrown itself. Many of its virtues are now held hostage to the amorphousness of the movement of which they are part, while its vices are increasingly apparent and subject to ridicule.

This book argues that defenders of cultural diversity need to take a step beyond multiculturalism, toward a perspective I call "postethnic." This perspective pulls together and defends certain elements of multiculturalism and criticizes others. A postethnic perspective favors voluntary over involuntary affiliations, balances an appreciation for communities of descent with a determination to make room for new communities, and promotes solidarities of wide scope that incorporate people with different ethnic and racial backgrounds. A postethnic perspective resists the grounding of knowledge and moral values in blood and history, but works within the last generation's recognition that many of the ideas and values once taken to be universal are specific to certain cultures. A postethnic perspective is not an all-purpose formula for solving policy problems, but it is a distinctive frame within which issues in education and politics can be debated.

A postethnic perspective builds upon a cosmopolitan element prominent within the multiculturalist movement and cuts against its equally prominent pluralist element. Multiculturalism is rent by an increasingly acute but rarely acknowledged tension between cosmopolitan and pluralist programs for the defense of cultural diversity. Pluralism respects inherited boundaries and locates individuals within one or another of a series of ethno-racial groups to be protected and preserved. Cosmopolitanism is more wary of traditional enclosures and favors voluntary affiliations. Cosmopolitanism promotes multiple identities, emphasizes the dynamic and changing character of many groups, and is responsive to the potential for creating new cultural combinations. Pluralism sees in cosmopolitanism a threat to identity, while cosmopolitanism sees in pluralism a provincial unwillingness to engage the complex dilemmas and opportunities actually presented by contemporary life.

But why call this cosmopolitan-inspired step beyond multiculturalism "postethnic"? Have we not too many "posts" already?

A *post*ethnic perspective develops and applies cosmopolitan ideals in a specific historical context: that of the past quarter-century's greater appreciation for a variety of kinds of *ethnic* connectedness. In contrast to the liberal critique of ethnocentrism prominent during the middle decades of the century, recent thinking about "community" has attributed to local, regional, religious, and ethno-racial units a capacity for the formation of human character said to be lacking in the national and global affiliations favored by universalists. Moreover, many ideas that were presented in the 1950s as "human nature" or "American culture" have turned out, under the critical scrutiny of historians, social scientists, and humanistic scholars, to be the particular interests of historically specific, empowered groups. Where all of humankind was once taken to be the referent, we are now more inclined to speak about, or on behalf of, an "ethnos," a particular solidarity rooted in history.

The term *postethnic* marks an effort to articulate and develop cosmopolitan instincts within this new appreciation for the ethnos. Cosmopolitanism itself is more generic. It is an impulse toward worldly breadth associated especially with the Enlightenment of the eighteenth century but found also in antiprovincial intellectuals in a host of times and places. As "citizens of the world," many of the great cosmopolitans of history have been proudly rootless. But postethnicity is the critical renewal of cosmopolitanism in the context of today's greater sensitivity to roots. "Rooted cosmopolitanism" is indeed a label recently adopted by several theorists of diversity whom I take to be moving in the direction I call postethnic.[1]

Hence the project of postethnicity differs decisively from many "posts" of our time. "Posting" is often a way of repudiating a preceding episode rather than building upon it and critically refining its contributions. Most vindications of postmodernism scorn modernism, or are condescending toward it. Instead, postethnicity is more respectful of ethnicity. The postethnic bears the same relation to the ethnic that post-Marxism bears to Marxism in the formulation of philosophers Ernesto Laclau and Chantal Mouffe: "But if our intellectual project . . . is *post*-Marxist, it is evidently also post-*Marxist*."[2] A postethnic perspective takes the claims of the ethnos more seriously than do recent, widely discussed critiques of epistemic particularism by Ernest Gellner and of civic particularism by Arthur M. Schlesinger, Jr.[3] Yet a postethnic perspective opens the possibility of a fresh dialogue with persons skeptical about some claims made in the name of multiculturalism. The critique of multiculturalism offered by Robert Hughes in his best-selling *The Culture of Complaint* is directed largely at the pluralist, rather than the cosmopolitan, strain of the movement.[4]

But the significance of the notion of postethnic should not be exaggerated. It refers to a cluster of insights and dispositions that are actually quite widespread in our time, especially in the writings of a number of people whom I cite in the pages of this book. I hope these ideas can play a greater role in our national—and international—conversation about diversity if they are identified, elaborated, and associated with a name. The word *postethnic*[5] is a practical linguistic device designed to stabilize and make more easily available a set of ideas that now flow in and out of multiculturalist discourse with the imperceptible ease of tidal waters in a lagoon. One can scarcely see the pluralists and the cosmopolitans coming and going because they all call themselves multiculturalists.

An example of how a postethnic perspective builds upon, rather than rejects, the ethnic is the postethnic emphasis on "affiliation." The preferred word in multiculturalist discourse is, of course, *identity*. But the concept of identity is more psychological than social, and it can hide the extent to which the achievement of identity is a social process by which a person becomes affiliated with one or more acculturating cohorts. In this respect, multiculturalism has not been ethnic enough: it has not developed a habit of speech that expresses its awareness of the importance of social groups to the lives of individuals. Moreover, the word *identity* implies fixity and givenness, while the word *affiliation* suggests a greater measure of flexibility consistent with a postethnic eagerness to promote communities of consent. Affiliation is more performative, while identity suggests something that simply is. To be sure, one can construe the achievement of identity as an action, but "affiliation" calls attention to the social dynamics of this action.

If our age is one in which the importance of group membership is more fully recognized, then we live in an age not of identities but of affiliations.[6] This is not to say that people do not have identities, including ethno-racial identities; nor is it to deny that individual identities can exploit in highly distinctive patterns the cultural inventories presented by the available communities. It is, instead, to underscore the simple fact that the identities people assume are acquired largely through affiliation, however prescribed or chosen.

The distinction between prescribed and chosen affiliations is the focal point of chapter 2 of *Postethnic America*. In the genealogical inquiry reported in his book *Roots,* Alex Haley might have chosen to trace his father's ancestry back to Ireland rather than his mother's back to Gambia. But this choice was phony, of course, for the blackness in Haley's

7

skin was understood to rule his white heritage inconsequential. Haley's choice is the Hobson's choice of ethno-racial identity in America because it is not a real choice at all. Although the lines that mark off other ethno-racial groups from one another are not as strictly enforced as those distinguishing white from black, residents of the United States are routinely asked to identify themselves and their contemporaries within one or another of five presumably involuntary communities of descent. This ethno-racial pentagon divides the population into African American, Asian American, Euro-American, Indigenous, and Latino segments, even as the labels for these five groups vary slightly. Fewer and fewer Americans believe in the biological reality of races, but they are remarkably willing to live with an officially sanctioned system of demographic classification that replicates precisely the crude, colloquial categories, black, yellow, white, red, and brown.

The ethno-racial pentagon won acceptance in the context of government efforts to prevent discrimination against minorities during the 1970s. But the multiculturalist movement of the following decade found the pentagon a convenient basis on which to organize the promotion of cultural diversity. A result was that categories deriving their integrity not from culture but from a history of political and economic victimization based on bad biology were frequently treated as cultures. When mixed-race people in the 1990s intensified protests against the confinements of the pentagon—demanding to be recognized as descendants of more than one of these communities—they brought the cultural and the political purposes of multiculturalism into a state of tragic contradiction. If a minority group were to lose members as a result of an exodus to the new mixed-race classification, the political clout of the group that loses its members would presumably diminish. The sharp increase in the numbers of avowedly mixed-race Americans also challenged the terms of Haley's choice and suggested that affiliation with a given community of descent could be more voluntary than ascribed. I argue for a sharper division of labor between the political and cultural aims that multiculturalism has blended together. I argue, also, that the concept of an "ethno-racial bloc" is more appropriate for today's antiracist discourse than the anachronistic term *race*, and I defend this view against those who resist the conflating of race and ethnicity.

Chapter 3 looks beyond the ethno-racial pentagon to a larger movement in recent history of which this pentagon is but one visible artifact: a transition from species-centered to ethnos-centered discourse in the history of the United States since World War II. Universalist aspirations were replaced by particularist aspirations in politics, social theory, anthropology, and other spheres of discussion. Nothing is more representative of this transition than the determination of today's thinkers to avoid an error they commonly attribute to their predecessors of the 1940s and 1950s: mistaking the local for the universal. A generation's well-meaning but unsuccessful efforts to address the species as a whole is now said to be visible in such classics of the era as the Kinsey reports on sexual behavior; Edward Steichen's photographic exhibit, *The Family of Man;* Wendell Willkie's exuberant prologue to the founding of the United Nations, *One World;* and Carey McWilliams's plea for integration, *Brothers under the Skin.* A chorus of voices now accuse that generation of ignoring difference and emphasizing sameness, of failing to see how different the various cultures of the world and of the nation are from each other. Some of these critiques are presented as postmodernist attacks on modernism, and, indeed, the species often turns out to hold the same relation to modernism that the ethnos does to postmodernism.

Some theorists defined basic standards for truth and goodness in relation to an ethnos. The name of the historian-philosopher Thomas S. Kuhn has become an emblem for an appreciation of the role of human communities in deciding just what ideas about nature shall count as scientific knowledge. If our judgments about what is scientifically valid and morally right have so much to do with the character of our communities, it is vital to be clear on just who "we" are. This question preoccupied a philosopher inspired by Kuhn, Richard Rorty, whose work I trace as a brief case study of the transition from species to ethnos.

Chapter 4 takes up the multiculturalist debates within the context of the larger species-to-ethnos transition charted in chapter 3. I provide examples of the different trajectories that are contained within multiculturalism, then develop in more detail the contrast mentioned above between pluralist and cosmopolitan elements within the movement. The words *pluralism* and *cosmopolitanism* have at times been assigned somewhat different meanings than the ones I use here, but I try to show why they are the most fair and efficient terms for the two orientations I want to distinguish. Part of this chapter is a historical overview of the background to multiculturalism, including the alliance of pluralism and cosmopolitanism against Anglo-conformist efforts to diminish cultural diversity.

The "cultural pluralism" associated with the name of Horace Kallen is an important precursor to multiculturalism. Kallen and his contemporary of the 1910s, the avowed cosmopolitan Randolph Bourne, are in some ways the models for the pluralist–cosmopolitan tension found in multiculturalism. Both share the basic idea that unites cultural pluralism with multiculturalism—that the nation should be home to a diversity of cultures, especially those carried by ethno-racial groups—but Bourne envisioned a dynamic interaction while Kallen stressed the autonomy of each group. The initiatives for tolerance and diversity during the 1940s, 1950s, and early 1960s largely ignored Kallen's cultural pluralism. The ideas of both Kallen and Bourne enjoy a revival within multiculturalism, but this new movement is much more popular than cultural pluralism had ever been. Indeed, the widespread triumph of the basic ideal of a culturally diverse America helped to bring the cosmopolitan and pluralist elements of the movement into greater tension with one another. In the meantime, multiculturalism's enthusiasm for diversity accelerated the articulation of difference to the point that diversity has become too diversified to be contained within the ethno-racial pentagon. The diversification of diversity and the increasingly visible frustration of the cosmopolitans within the movement are both incentives to develop a postethnic perspective.

Sketching that perspective is the business of chapter 5. In keeping with lessons learned from the diversification of diversity, the postethnic perspective recognizes the instrumental character and the varying size, scope, and purposes of the communities within which people work out their politics, their values, their standards for truth, and their personal identities. Any individual's life-project will entail a shifting division of labor between the various overlapping "we's" of which he or she is a part. A postethnic perspective thus resists the pluralist temptation to depict society as an expanse of internally homogeneous and analogically structured units, each possessed of a comparable myth of diaspora. A postethnic perspective is alert for opportunities to construct global solidarities capable of addressing ecological and other dilemmas that are global in their impact. A postethnic perspective favors expanding the epistemic "we"—the community upon which we depend for scientific knowledge—as far as the capacities of nature and its inquirers will allow. Here, I allude to relevant work by recent historians and philosophers of science. So, too, do I identify work of recent moral theorists that promotes a stretching of the moral "we" in realistic dialogue with people who begin with values very different from "ours."

A postethnic perspective on communities of descent within the United States entails the principle of affiliation by revocable consent. This modest choice-maximizing principle supports the renewal and critical revision of those communities of descent whose progeny choose to devote their energies to these communities even after experiencing opportunities for affiliating with other kinds of people. A postethnic perspective denies neither history nor biology, nor the need for affiliations, but it does deny that history and biology provide a set of clear orders for the affiliations we are to make. The postethnic preference for choice over prescription favors a sharper distinction than multiculturalists often make between *cultures* and the specifically *ethno-racial classifications* often said to be the indicators of the boundaries of a culture. "Culture" has often turned out to be a euphemism for "ethnicity" or "race." There is plenty of culture to be studied and appreciated within all of the social spaces marked off by the standard ethno-racial categories. But multiculturalism affords little recognition to culture that transcends these categories and comes in packages that have little to do with ethno-racial communities. I urge more attention to religiously defined cultures and suggest some of the consequences of looking upon religious groups as "ethnic" and upon ethnic groups as "religious." The prevailing bias toward ethno-racial constructions of culture is also apparent in the reluctance of many multiculturalists to attribute culture to the transethnic community that is the topic of chapter 6, the United States itself.

A postethnic perspective on American nationality emphasizes the civic character of the American nation-state, in contrast to the ethnic character of most of the nationalism we read about today. A civic nation can mediate between the species and the ethnos in ways that an ethnic nation cannot. In the context of the worldwide resurgence of ethno-racial particularism, the transethnic solidarity of the American civic nation has much to recommend it. The United States, as a civic nation with an ethno-racially diverse population, mediates more directly than most nations do between the species and the varieties of humankind. I argue that the value of civic nation-states in protecting rights and providing basic welfare is undervalued by proponents of postnationality. Against the view that the United States is more a container of ethno-racially defined cultures than a basis for an ethnos of its own, I defend the notion of a national culture as an adhesive enabling diverse Americans to see themselves as sufficiently "in it together" to act on problems that are genuinely common. Recognition of the reality of a national culture also saves the United States from the dangerous conceit that it is a proto-world-state. Affirming the particularity of American culture need not be an act of arrogance; rather, it can be an act of humility in the face of the world's diversity.

The American nation-state is being pulled in different directions by three formidable constituencies. One is a business elite that, in an age of international corporations, finds more and more of its employees and factories abroad. This elite has some need for the American state, but it can get along without attending very carefully to the needs of the nation, the people who constitute the community of American citizens. The second constituency identifies with one or more diasporas and sees the United States more as a site for transnational affiliations than as an affiliation of its own. The proponents of diasporic consciousness sometimes look to the state as a source of entitlements, but, like the business elite, they have little incentive to devote themselves to the welfare of the national community. In the meantime, a third constituency has claimed America with a vengeance. This third constituency is made up of a great variety of Middle Americans, evangelical Christians, advocates of family values, and supporters of Newt Gingrich and of Rush Limbaugh. Many of these Americans are suspicious of the state except as an enforcer of personal morality, but they claim the nation as, in effect, their own ethnic group. The ideological resources of the American nation-state are too valuable to multiculturalists to be allowed to fall, by default, into the hands of this third constituency, which most multiculturalists see as their enemy. Being an American amid a multiplicity of affiliations need not be threatening to cultural diversity, nor need it be too shallow an identity to partake of a vital solidarity of its own.

Although I take a more generous view of the American nation-state and of the culture that has developed around it than is usually expressed by active defenders of cultural diversity, this book is far from cheerful, either about America or about the prospects for the postethnic ideal. In the epilogue, I express my fear that the United States, by failing to provide sufficient opportunities for poor people of all ethno-racial affiliations, is in the process of squandering whatever opportunity it may now have to move in a more postethnic direction.

The deepest problems within the United States are masked, it is asserted with increasing frequency, by culture wars that direct public attention toward the discussion of cultural reforms that are relatively inexpensive and hold scant promise to reduce inequality.[7] The multiculturalist movement itself, it is also suggested more and more often, has hurt its own cause by indulging in silly and authoritarian tactics.[8] There is much truth in both of these charges. But behind multiculturalism and the mistakes made in its name remain questions about the nation's character too relevant to public policy to be thrust aside in a spasm of frustration. The United States will be better able to address its economic and political inequalities, and to maintain its civil libertarian traditions, if it can achieve a more satisfactory perspective on cultural issues while not inflating their significance. That is what this book tries to do.

CHAPTER 2

Haley's Choice and the Ethno-racial Pentagon

"If Alex Haley had traced his father's bloodline, he would have traveled twelve generations back to, not Gambia, but *Ireland*," Ishmael Reed has observed of Haley's *Roots*.[1] Haley's choice of roots is an emblem for three points that drive this book: the United States is endowed with a *non*ethnic ideology of the nation; it is possessed by a predominantly *ethnic* history; and it may now be squandering an opportunity to create for itself a *post*ethnic future in which affiliation on the basis of shared descent would be more voluntary than prescribed.

The national ideology is nonethnic by virtue of the universalist commitment—proclaimed in the Constitution and the prevailing political discourse—to provide the benefits of citizenship irrespective of any ascribed or asserted ancestral affiliations. This commitment lies behind our sense that

Haley had a real choice, and one that was his to make: individual Americans are to be as free as possible from the consequences of social distinctions visited upon them by others. Yet the decision Haley made was driven by a history predominantly ethnic in the extent to which each American's individual destiny has been determined by ancestrally derived distinctions. These distinctions have been flagged, at one time or another, by such labels as Negro, Jewish, Indian, Caucasian, Hispanic, Indigenous, Oriental, Irish, Italian, Chinese, Polish, white, black, Latino, Euro-American, Native American, Chicano, and African American.[2] That any person now classified as black or African American might see his or her own life as more the product of African roots—however small or large a percentage of one's actual, biological genealogy and cultural experience—than of European roots reflects this history.[3]

Hence Haley's choice is the Hobson's choice of genealogy in America. Haley could choose to identify with Africa, accepting, in effect, the categories of the white oppressors who had determined that the tiniest fraction of African ancestry would confer one identity and erase another. Or, Haley could choose to identify with Ireland, denying, in effect, his solidarity with people who most shared his social destiny. The nature of this choice is further illuminated by an experience reported by Reed, whose ancestry is also African and Irish, and who has flirted with the other option in the structured dilemma I am calling Haley's choice.

Reed mentioned his "Irish-American heritage" to a "Professor of Celtic Studies at Dartmouth," who "laughed."[4]

In a postethnic America someone of Reed's color could march in a St. Patrick's Day parade without anyone finding it a joke. A postethnic America would offer Haley a choice more real than the one Hobson gave visitors to his stable when he told them that they could take any horse they wanted as long as it was the one nearest the door. And postethnicity would enable Haley and Reed to be both African American and Irish American without having to choose one to the exclusion of the other. Postethnicity reacts against the nation's invidiously ethnic history, builds upon the current generation's unprecedented appreciation of previously ignored cultures, and supports on the basis of revocable consent those affiliations by shared descent that were previously taken to be primordial.

Although this ideal gains some credibility in the context of the recent efforts of mixed-race Americans to defy traditional classifications, the notion of a postethnic America is deeply alien to many features of American and world history. This notion exists in uneasy tension, moreover, with a contemporary system of entitlements predicated on clear, enduring, and monolithic ethno-racial identities. Hence the exploration of the postethnic ideal needs to begin by underscoring the inequalities that have dominated the historical record[5] and recognizing that these inequalities lend credibility to claims made on behalf of communities defined by descent.

Not every citizen's fortunes have been influenced to the same degree, or in the same direction, by America's notorious failure to act on its universalist aspirations. Being classified as Euro-American, white, or Caucasian has rarely been a basis for being denied adequate employment, housing, education, or protection from violence. One response to the patently unequal consequences of ethno-racial distinctions has been to invoke and sharpen the nation's official, Enlightenment-derived commitment to protect all its citizens from them. What this commitment means has been contested, of course, from the day a committee of the Second Continental Congress deleted from the Declaration of Independence Thomas Jefferson's denunciation of slavery to the most recent decisions of the United States Supreme Court concerning the limits of affirmative action. The commitment is plain enough, however, to make obvious the gap between the theory and the practice of American nationality.[6] Indeed, the magnitude and persistence of this gap have inspired a second, very different response: pressure from the gap's other side, its ethnic side.

This alternative strategy for closing the gap asks public authority to facilitate and actively support affiliation on the basis of ancestry. By promoting the development of communities defined by descent, one might reasonably hope for more equal treatment of every descendant of every tribe. After all, the results produced by the long-preferred method of closing gaps—invoking and sharpening the nonethnic ideological tradition—remain disappointing even to most people who believe progress has been substantial. The nonethnic character of the ideological tradition can be construed as part of the problem rather than part of the solution. That tradition treats as irrelevant to citizenship the very distinctions that, in this newer view, need to be asserted, reinforced, and celebrated. Policies that ignore the distinctions now called "ethnic" or "racial" may place at a disadvantage people whose physical appearance, social behavior, or cultural tastes lead others to classify them ethno-racially, and then to discriminate against them in keeping with prevailing prejudice.

This feeling—that the goal of equality demands for America a future even more ethnic than its past—has encouraged the nation to accept a distinctive system of classification by descent-defined communities. This is the set of categories Americans most often confront when asked to identify themselves by a multitude of public and private agencies. On application forms and questionnaires, individuals are routinely invited to declare themselves to be one of the following: Euro-American (or sometimes white), Asian American, African American, Hispanic (or sometimes Latino), and Indigenous Peoples (or sometimes Native American). To gain a clearer understanding of this five-part demographic structure and of the pressures now being brought against it is the chief concern of this chapter.

The ethno-racial pentagon, as we might call it, is a

remarkable historical artifact, distinctive to the contemporary United States. The five specified blocs are not equally populated or empowered, but the five-part structure itself is supposed to embrace us all. This structure might also be called a "quintuple melting pot," replacing the "triple melting pot" made famous by Will Herberg's book of 1955, *Protestant-Catholic-Jew*.[7] The distinctions between white Jews, white Catholics, and white Protestants that Herberg and his contemporaries thought so important have now diminished. The elements in each segment of the new structure do "melt" to some extent, but the old figure of the melting pot does not capture the process by which individuals are assigned space on the basis of their perceived communities of descent. Today's device for classification is not even a guide to lines along which genealogical interaction and merging are taking place; rather, it is a framework for politics and culture in the United States. It is an implicit prescription for the principles on which Americans should maintain communities; it is a statement that certain affiliations matter more than others.

Although this ethno-racial pentagon is now visible in many places, it is not the only demographic blueprint now being used. One competitor is defined by the term *people of color*. In this view, white and nonwhite are the two relevant categories, and all distinctions between various "colored" peoples are less significant than the fact that they are nonwhite. But it is the ethno-racial penta-gon, not the color-noncolor dichotomy, that public and private agencies most often ask residents of the United States to locate themselves within. A major difference between the two systems of classification concerns cul-ture. The white-colored dichotomy does not have a strong cultural content, but the ethno-racial pentagon does, and increasingly so, especially for educational pur-poses. An example is the widely publicized decision made in 1989 by the faculty of the University of California at Berkeley to require undergraduates to take a course involving the comparative study of at least three of five American cultures. The three were to be selected from the five blocs in the ethno-racial pentagon.[8]

The pentagon, in its capacity as guide to the cultural life of the United States, has symbolically erased much of the cultural diversity within the Euro-American bloc. The category of Euro-American, observed a journalist con-cerned with Irish American identity, has accomplished in short order a task that centuries of British imperial power could not complete: making the Irish indistinguishable from the English.[9] Jewish identity, too, receded in signifi-cance when all Americans of predominantly European stock were grouped together. To be sure, a value of the pentagon is its capacity to call attention to a certain range of social and cultural diversity. But as is so often the case when the virtues of difference are contrasted to the vices of sameness, at issue is not really difference in general but the highlighting of certain differences at the expense of others.

Indeed, this diminution of the differences between various groups of Euro-Americans has dramatized the contingent, contextual character of the entire process by which differences and similarities are created, perpetuated, and altered. A New Hampshire resident of French Canadian ethnicity may learn, by moving to Texas, that he or she is actually an Anglo. Many European immigrants of the nineteenth century did not come to see themselves as significantly Italian or German until these identities were thrust upon them by the novel demographic conditions of the United States, which rendered obsolete the local identities into which they had been acculturated in Sicily and Swabia. Distinctions between Protestants, Catholics, and Jews of European extraction were once taken as seriously in the United States as are the distinctions now made between Euro-Americans and Asian Americans. Although the insight that ethno-racial distinctions are socially constructed is rapidly gaining ground, it is still obliged to struggle against popular, deeply entrenched assumptions that ethno-racial groups are primordial in foundation.

The sudden transformation of a great number of distinctive ethnic identities into Euro-America ought to make white Americans more sensitive to the comparable erasures of diversity that attend on the other four, pseudoprimal categories, some of which have been sanctioned by longer use. Tribal and linguistic distinctions among Native American peoples have long been lost on many non-Indian observers. The identity one attributes to Americans whose ancestors were Koreans, Cambodians, Chinese, Vietnamese, and Japanese by calling them all Asian Americans (or, in the older usage, Orientals) is obtained by diminishing the differences between them and other Americans of Asian extraction. The Hispanic, or Latino, bloc has more linguistic cohesion than does the Asian American or the Indigenous Peoples bloc, but it, too, can be broken down into subgroups defined, for example, by such points of origin as Argentina, Cuba, El Salvador, Mexico, and Puerto Rico.

The internal diversity of the African American bloc may be the least obvious, as measured by linguistic distinctions and national origins. Nothing, however, illustrates the selective suppression of diversity and the socially constructed character of these ethno-racial blocs more tellingly than the historic denial, by generations of empowered whites, that they share with black Americans a substantial pool of genes. As historian Barbara Fields has put the point, we still have a convention "that considers a white woman capable of giving birth to a black child but denies that a black woman can give birth to a white child."[10] The persistence of the "one-drop rule" deprives those with any hint of black skin of any choice in their ethno-racial affiliation. It makes a mockery of the idea that the ethno-racial pentagon is simply a realistic response to the facts of genealogical life, a set of five gardens each providing natural and sustaining roots. Hence, Haley's choice.

And it is choice, so highly valued by the postethnic perspective, that is so severely limited by this pentagon. A Cambodian American does not have to remain Cambodian, as far as non–Asian Americans are concerned, but only with great difficulty can this Cambodian American cease to be an Asian American. So, too, with Japanese Americans or Chinese Americans. As was implicitly asked by the white autoworker from Detroit who in 1982 clubbed to death the Chinese American Vincent Chin, thinking him Japanese, "What's the difference, anyway?" The same applies to the other blocs: indigenous peoples might care who is a Cherokee and who is a Kwakiutl, but outside that section of the pentagon, an Indian is usually an Indian. Some Jewish Americans might take great pride in their particularity as Jews, but from the viewpoint of many African Americans— returning an old favor—it is the whiteness of the whole lot of them that counts. And so on. Moreover, the Bureau of the Census allows the selection of one ethno-racial category and prohibits the choice of more than one.

The lines between the five unequally inhabited sides of the ethno-racial pentagon mark the limits of individual movement, as set by prevailing convention. The several lines distinguishing one segment of the pentagon from another are not resistant in exactly the same degree to intermarriage and other types of border crossing and category mixing. Yet, all are strong enough to function as "racial" as opposed to "ethnic" boundaries. Two kinds of lines are, in fact, being drawn, and they are widely accepted, at least for now: fainter lines distinguish the ethnicities found *within* each of the five blocs (Swedes, Filipinos, Pawnees, etc.), while bolder, thicker lines render the five blocs themselves into races, or race equivalents.

The ethno-racial pentagon is a highly particular creation of recent American history, although it draws upon traditional races. Some of the blocs owe much more than others do to classical race theory of the nineteenth century. Two "races" included in most of those old, now anachronistic schemas—some of which posited the existence of only three or four races, and others of which listed dozens—were called Mongoloid and Negroid, obviously prefiguring the Asian American and African American blocs. But the American adherence to the one-drop rule renders the African American bloc a distinctive formation, unlike the categories traditionally employed in Brazil, South Africa, and elsewhere to recognize racial mixture. Moreover, Mongoloid was generally taken to encompass only the peoples of east Asia, not those of south Asia now routinely included in the Asian American segment of the pentagon. When Mongoloid was construed by race theorists as a broader category, it embraced not the Hindus of south Asia or the Persians of central Asia but the original population of the Western Hemisphere, who, according to some other schemes, were a separate American race. The latter prefigured the Native American or Indigenous bloc.

The Euro-American bloc is obviously derived from the white category, but the American sense of whiteness was not simply an application of the Caucasian of classical race theory. Immigrants from India were undoubtedly Caucasians according to physical anthropologists in the early twentieth century, but the United States Supreme Court ruled in 1923 that south Asian immigrants and their descendants were sufficiently "nonwhite" to be ineligible for naturalization as whites.[11] Jews from Europe and elsewhere were sometimes said to be a separate race. Even European immigrant groups whose whiteness was not legally contested—those from Ireland, Italy, and Poland, for example—were long considered so different that the significance of their whiteness diminished except in contexts when black-skinned people were present. The category of "white people" was articulated in the modern United States primarily in relation to black people and secondarily in relation to people of other colors. It took on greater significance as more and more European immigrant groups consolidated their political and economic connections with the Anglo-Protestant population so obviously in control of American institutions.[12]

"White" is a dehistoricized and culturally vacant category, while "Euro-American" invokes something at least slightly more specific. When voices representing the nonwhite affiliations placed greater emphasis on the cultural component of each of these groups in keeping with the multiculturalism of the 1980s and 1990s, the notion that whites should be comparably particularized as Euro-Americans made better and better sense. The linguistic move from *white* to *Euro-American,* inspired in part by the increasing popularity of *African American* to replace *black* and even *Afro-American,* symbolically cut down to size the whites who would otherwise continue to be anomalously unhistoricized. Whites, too, were migrants from elsewhere to what is now the United States, and thus deserving of a hyphen indicating their point of origin. The transition from "white" to "Euro-American" thus partakes of the particularizing dynamic that has made the ethno-racial pentagon a more sharply defined feature of American life.

The bloc that owes the least to classical race theory is the Hispanic, or Latino, bloc. The various peoples now grouped in this bloc were usually considered white, or Caucasian, until only the last two decades. Also, they were commonly designated by country of origin—Mexico, Cuba, Puerto Rico, etc.—much the way European ethnics were associated with either Italy or Poland or Denmark. "Brown" remained only a colloquial designation, although it served to mark lines of discrimination in many communities, especially in California and Texas. As late as the 1990 census, more than half of the Mexican American population continued to classify itself as white. This notion of the whiteness of Hispanic ethnics has prevailed despite the recognition that the ancestry of the people of Mexico was heavily indigenous and that the population of Puerto Rico consisted largely of a mixture of white and black ancestry in a combination anomalously exempted from the American one-drop rule. A sign of the consolidation of the ethnoracial pentagon, however, is the increasing frequency with which the people in this Latino bloc are being called a "race" in popular discourse.

This gradual racialization of Latinos completes, in turn, the process by which the blocs of the pentagon, whatever their shifting labels, have come to replicate the popular color-consciousness of the past: black, white, red, yellow, and brown. If the classical race theory of the nineteenth century is not directly behind the pentagon, this structure's architecture has its unmistakable origins in the most gross and invidious of popular images of what makes human beings different from one another.

Yet it was enlightened antiracism that led to the manufacturing of today's ethno-racial pentagon out of old, racist materials. The most immediate force behind the creation of the pentagon has been the antidiscrimination and affirmative action policies of the federal government. Reliable statistics were required to enforce the Voting Rights Act of 1965. It was difficult to protect black people from being disenfranchised without census data revealing the extent and exact location of their exclusion from voting. The same dynamic applied to employment discrimination; pools of candidates identified by ethno-racial category had to be available to facilitate enforcement of Title VII of the Civil Rights Act of 1964. Affirmative action runs on numbers. In this context, the single event most responsible for the lines that separate one bloc from another was the issuing in 1977 of what seemed to be a modest directive by the Office of Management and Budget designed to enable government workers to collect needed information.

Statistical Directive 15 of this office of the federal bureaucracy instructed federal agencies to classify people racially as white, black, American Indian, and Asian or Pacific Islander, and to distinguish within the white race between those of Hispanic and those of non-Hispanic origin. Although the words commonly used to denote these groups have shifted somewhat during the years since 1977, and still vary somewhat from context to context, the five blocs of the pentagon are clearly visible in this administrative directive. That it makes sense to call these blocs race equivalents is borne out by the demand of the National Council of La Raza that the Census Bureau reclassify Hispanics as a race rather than merely an ethnic group for the census to be taken in the year 2000.[13]

Exactly where ethnicity ends and race begins has been much contested in our time, when zoologists and anthropologists have found so little scientific utility in the concept of race,[14] and when humanists and social scientists have found so much evidence for the socially constructed character of race as well as ethnicity. Classifying people by the physical marks that distinguished the races, the philosopher Anthony Appiah has pointed out, was "like trying to classify books in a library" on the basis of size and shape.[15] Only a tiny fraction of a person's genetic inheritance, like a tiny fraction of a book's character, is taken into account by such a mode of classification. Yet the term *race* continues to have great currency, even among people who deny that races exist as anthropological entities and who know that genetic variation from one race to another is scarcely greater than genetic variation within the races. Two of the most eloquent of these nonbelievers in race, Henry Louis Gates, Jr., and Tzvetan Todorov, have carried on a vehement debate over whether the word *race* should be placed in quotation marks within the pages of a book about the role of race in literature, the contributors to which agreed that there was no such thing as race.[16]

A host of critics warn against the conflating of race with ethnicity on the grounds that a vital distinction would be lost. But the continued use of the word *race* to distinguish the groups of the pentagon, or indeed to distinguish any groups of people from one another in any context whatsoever, is highly problematic from a postethnic perspective. Does this usage serve the ultimate interest of diminishing the deleterious effects of ascribed distinctions, and does it encourage affiliation on the basis of revocable consent? I think not. I want to explain why the term *ethno-racial bloc,* however awkward it sounds, is a more accurate representation than *race* of what antiracists mean today when we refer to African Americans, Euro-Americans, and the other three groups recognized by the pentagon.

When we now refer to a race, we most often mean to address the unequal treatment of people on the basis of biological ideas long since discredited. The paradigm case is that of black people, whose mistreatment by white people in the history of this society has been so conspicuous, so enduring, so closely tied to biological ideas, and has affected so large a segment of the population of the United States. The concept of race appears to help us identify a population that Europeans and white Americans have (1) classified as different from themselves on the basis of certain physical characteristics—especially skin color, hair, and shape of the face—and (2) treated less generously than they have treated other Europeans and white Americans. This treatment has been based largely on the false belief that these physical differences were the causes of behavioral and cultural traits that the Europeans and white Americans did not like. We also use race to identify the one community of descent most responsible for these classifications and for the unequal treatment justified by them, the Caucasians or Europeans. The concept of race, then, serves us reasonably well when we want to be aware of a pattern of behavior: it refers to the lines along which people have been systematically mistreated on the basis of certain physical characteristics.

Race does not serve us at all well, however, when we want to talk about culture. Although the pentagon has been taken up by multiculturalism as a convenient basis for organizing the defense of cultural diversity, the lines dividing the five parts of the pentagon are not designed to recognize coherent cultures. They are designed, instead, to correct injustices committed by white people in the name of the American nation, most but not all of which can be traced back to racial classifications on the basis of morphological traits. Culture abounds within all five blocs of the pentagon, and much of it has been created under circumstances of victimization and its memory. But even if the several blocs are understood as spaces relevant to the creation of culture and as rough groupings of specific cultural units, the fact remains that culture is more relevant to the faint lines that divide the ethnicities within each of the blocs than it is to the lines that divide the blocs from one another. Americans of Japanese, Navajo, or French descent can all claim a more particular cultural inheritance than can be reasonably ascribed to Asian Americans, Indigenous Peoples, or Euro-Americans in general. The tendency to treat the blocs of the pentagon as cultural rather than political categories risks saddling us with a sense of diversity grounded in an analysis not of cultural difference but of the history of victimization justified largely by what we now recognize to be biologically superficial differentiators of human groups.

When it is said that race affects one's destiny more than ethnicity does, the reference usually turns out to be to different degrees of mistreatment within a social system, not to different degrees of cultural particularity and group enforcement of norms. Some of the various ethnic groups within the Euro-American bloc have had their share of suffering, but it is dwarfed, according to our common if not always stated understanding, by the suffering inflicted on races. Moreover, the Chinese American suffers less as a Chinese than as an Asian, just as the Crow suffers not as a Crow but as an Indian. Although Japanese Americans were interned during World War II as Japanese rather than as Asians, that Asianness made the difference is proven by the less harsh treatment afforded Americans of highly visible German or Italian affiliations. This distinction between degrees of victimization is the key to the place of Latinos in the ethno-racial pentagon and to the assertion of a racial status on their behalf.[17]

Since the 1970s, Latinos have won more widespread recognition as a historically disadvantaged minority that has suffered wrongs comparable to those suffered by the minority groups earlier called races. These wrongs include discriminatory acts by whites in the twentieth-century United States, but in the background is a slavery equivalent. This is the annexation of what is now the southwestern section of the United States from Mexico in 1848. This conquest is said to confer upon even recent immigrants from parts of Mexico not conquered by the United States the status of an American-oppressed minority. Hence the logic of racial distinctions comes to embrace Latinos—including, by indirection, immigrants from El Salvador and Venezuela, countries that felt the force of American imperialism even less directly—despite the traditional Latino self-conception as non-Anglo white. Even if the victimization is symbolic, it is the victimization that counts.

The way this system of classification works can be further illustrated by comparing the status of Latinos with that of Jewish Americans. Jews were once widely thought of as a race, but are no longer. This transformation did not result primarily from scientific advances in biology and physical anthropology. Rather, the prejudice against Jewish Americans within American historical experience is judged to be less severe and damaging than the prejudice against Latinos, who, because of that greater perceived victimization, are now said to constitute a race. When we caution ourselves not to ignore race by conflating race and ethnicity, we generally mean to remind ourselves of the sharpest inequalities of treatment within the American nation-state or in direct relation to its conduct in the larger world.[18]

Hence, the blocs of the pentagon get their integrity not from biology, nor even from culture, but from the dynamics of prejudice and oppression in U.S. history and from the need for political tools to overcome the legacy of that victimization. *Race* may be a word we are stuck with, but there are sound reasons to resist its continued use as an unmodified noun. The notion of race was originally developed to refer to the deeply structural differences between human groups; these differences were understood to be both highly determinative of human character and immutable, as in the old figure of speech, "the leopard cannot change his spots." Yet now, paradoxically, we rely upon the word *race* to mark something virtually antithetical: identities created by patterns in human *conduct* that we take to be *changeable,* indeed, exactly the ones we would *most* like to change, namely, the patterns of unequal treatment according to perceived descent. The word *racism* still works splendidly to indicate this pattern of unequal treatment.

The parties to this interaction that are still commonly called races I prefer to subsume under the more general category ethno-racial blocs.[19] This phrasing better reflects our understanding of the contingent and instrumental character of the categories, acknowledges that the groups traditionally called racial exist on a blurred continuum with those traditionally called ethnic, and more easily admits the renunciation, once and for all, of the unequal treatment in America of human beings on the basis of the marks of descent once called racial. Changing our vocabulary will not do much to diminish unequal treatment, but it might at least keep us aware of the direction in which antiracists want to be heading. Racism is real, but races are not.

Real, too, are differences from bloc to bloc in the degree of freedom individuals have to choose how much or how little emphasis to place on their community of descent. Nowhere within the entire ethno-racial pentagon do individuals have more of this freedom than within the Euro-American bloc. The ease with which American whites can affirm or ignore their ethnic identity as Italians, Norwegians, Irish, and so on has often been noted by sociologists, and was convincingly documented by Mary C. Waters in her 1990 book, *Ethnic Options: Choosing Identities in America*. Many middle-class Americans of third- or fourth-generation immigrant descent get a great deal of satisfaction out of their ethnic affiliations, which, in the current cultural and political environment, cost them little.[20] Waters found that these white ethnics tended to avoid aspects of communal life that imposed obligations and intruded on their privacy and individuality. They affirmed what the sociologist Herbert Gans calls "symbolic ethnicity." They take pleasure in a subjective feeling of ethnic identity, but shy away from the more substantive ethnicity that demands involvement in a concrete community with organizations, mutual commitments, and some elements of constraint.[21]

Although Waters found abundant evidence for the voluntary character of the ethnicity affirmed by middle-class whites, she also encountered among these manifestly voluntary ethnics the persistent notion that ethnicity is a primordial, biological status. Her subjects' denial of the voluntary character of their own ethnic identities rendered them, in turn, insensitive to the difference between their own situation and that of Americans with non-European ethno-racial identities. These whites see a formal "equivalence between the African-American and, say, Polish-American heritages." Thus, they deny, in effect, the depth and durability of the racism that has largely constructed and persistently bedeviled the African American and rendered that heritage less voluntary than an affirmation of Polishness.[22] Waters's subjects do not understand, one might say, the distinction between the blocs of the pentagon and the ethnicities nested within the blocs.

Waters's book is intended, in part, to liberate white Americans from these blindnesses, which help to prevent many nonwhite Americans from enjoying the freedom now experienced by whites to affiliate and disaffiliate at will. When Waters argues for such a consummation—a time when "all Americans" are equally "free to exercise their 'ethnic option'"—she upholds the ideal I am calling postethnic.[23] In such a consummation, the vividly etched lines that define the five sections of the ethno-racial pentagon would be fainter, more like the lines internal to each of the five segments. By contrast, an ethnic America would present us with what we have already had, only more so: the lines now vivid would become even more sharply drawn, and the lines now faint would become more bold.

Uncertain as the future is, there is no doubt that the

ethno-racial pentagon is now being placed under severe pressure by the rate of intermarriage and by the greater visibility of mixed-race people. The conventional term *mixed race* perpetuates the anachronism of race I quarreled with above. But here the retention of the word *race* actually serves to convey more dramatically than *bloc* the depth of the challenge presented to the system by people whose proclaimed descent lies in more than one of the segments of the pentagon. Between a quarter and a third of all marriages involving Japanese Americans are now out-group marriages. More indigenous people marry outside the Indigenous bloc than marry within it. Even marriages between African Americans and whites, prohibited in some states as late as the 1960s, have increased by 300 percent since 1970.[24] A society long hostile to racial mixture, and exceptionally skilled at denying its reality, now confronts a rapidly increasing population of avowedly mixed-race families and individuals.

And it is the avowal that matters, even more than the numbers. Organizations advancing the distinctive interests of mixed-race peoples have multiplied in recent years and often lobby the Bureau of the Census to recognize them as a distinctive ethno-racial group of their own. The significance of the increase in cross-bloc mixtures consists also in the specific kinds of mixtures that now demand public acceptance. Asian European mixtures are highly visible because the society does not have a long-standing convention of concealing them by automatically consigning them to the Asian side of the descent, as it consigns black-white mixtures to the black side. Moreover, Asians have been more widely understood to be a race than Latinos have been, with the result that Asian European mixtures are, again, more dramatic challenges to the system than have been Latino European mixtures. Mexican Americans, in particular, have long embodied and taken for granted a mixed ancestry. Yet in the present climate this tradition of mixture, as it is reaffirmed and proclaimed, also contributes to the challenge being mounted against the constraints of the pentagon. "By merely reaffirming their heritage," suggests Carlos Fernandez, Mexican Americans are "uniquely positioned to upset the traditional Anglo-American taboo" against mixing.[23]

The most potent threat to the ethno-racial pentagon is probably the increase in avowed double minorities and multiple minorities. People whose descent is divided between African American and one or more of the other non-Euro-American blocs represent a special challenge to the terms of Haley's choice. The phenomenon of the double minority is not new. But persons of mixed African American and either indigenous or Latino descent were traditionally classified as belonging to any one or another of these three blocs, depending on the immediate social environment. The one-drop rule was sometimes quietly compromised when non-Euro-American people were involved. But this compromise has become less quiet in the wake of two developments.

First, the greater pride taken in indigenous and Latino as well as African American descent in recent years has made more compelling the claims of each descent on any individual who happens to be heir to more than one of them. If the affirmation of a white heritage has traditionally risked bringing upon anyone of partially African American descent the charge of denying solidarity with black people and "wanting to be white," this difficulty diminishes with double minorities. The difficulty is not altogether absent in the case of affirmation of Latino descent, but now that Latinos, whether white or not, are in possession of their own race-equivalent bloc in the pentagon, the problem is smaller. Nor does the difficulty raised by "wanting to be white" loom large in the affirmation of safely nonwhite indigenous descent.

Second, there has recently emerged for the first time on a demographically significant scale a new kind of double minority: Asian African. The mixed-race individuals who lobby the most adamantly for a new census category to accommodate them are often Asian-African-Americans.

If the one-drop rule ever falls, it is mostly likely to do so under the specific pressure brought upon it by double and multiple minorities, who may then create an atmosphere in which this rule can weaken elsewhere, even where it now serves to separate the Euro-American and the African American segments of the pentagon. Even now, this strongest of all ethno-racial barriers is being chipped away as individuals of white and African American mixture are heard more frequently in public hearings trying to defy the one-drop rule.[26]

While the demand to add mixed race to the federal census can be construed as merely an effort to turn the pentagon into a hexagon, the logic of mixed race actually threatens to destroy the whole structure. A concern for the political cohesion of the African American bloc, in particular, has led a number of scholars and activists to resist this innovation. "Instead of draining the established categories of their influence," a writer for the *New Yorker* recently found some African American intellectuals in the process of concluding, "it would be better to eliminate racial categories altogether."[27] The various blocs of the pentagon are literally filled with mixed-race people.[28] Although this fact is noted the most often in regard to the African American bloc for which Alex Haley is so convenient a symbol, it is also visible in the Indigenous bloc, where it has reached the point of a statistical apocalypse.

Tribal governments, which are legally empowered to decide who shall be counted as a member of any given tribe, apply radically divergent standards. At least one tribal government will enroll "those with 1/256 Indian blood heritage," reports Terry Wilson, while other tribal governments demand "one-half quantum from the *mother's* heritage," and still others follow an old practice of the U.S. government, classifying as Indian anyone with one-quarter indigenous ancestry.[29] In the meantime, no individual needs to obtain tribal authorization to self-identify on a census form as a member of the American Indian race. Thousands of Americans who had never before declared themselves to be indigenous peoples have done so in recent censuses in response, presumably, to the promise of entitlements and to the cultural reality of more positive public attitudes toward Indians. The number of Americans who identified themselves as American Indians on federal census forms increased by 259 percent between 1960 and 1990.[30]

Some whites, in the meantime, have insisted that they are black. Opportunities for self-identification have produced a statistically tiny but administratively portentous effort to enter the African American bloc for the purpose of exploiting entitlement programs designed for minorities. The most notorious case involves two brothers—Paul and Philip Malone—who obtained employment in the Boston fire department in 1977 by self-identifying as black even though, as the state supreme court of Massachusetts ruled in 1989, they had declared themselves to be black solely for the purpose of gaining employment for which their test scores as whites had been too low to qualify.[31] Although such cases might seem to be easily resolvable at the level of common sense, the question of who is a real minority can be highly frustrating when it comes to establishing clear and equitable legal rules for making the determination.

To what extent should self-identification be supplemented by the opinions of a larger community? And should that community consist of obvious members of the entitlement-targeted population in question, or of members of the groups most likely to be guilty of the discrimination against which the entitlement programs are directed? Legal scholar Christopher Ford finds these questions demanding of much more attention than American jurisprudence has so far provided. It makes some sense to let each group decide who is in and who is out, but there are limits to this approach. "Since the distribution of racial disadvantage is presumably keyed by how the *rest of society* perceives the claimant," Ford observes, the standards for identifying a black person that obtain outside the black community would

> appear the most likely to target remedy to wrong: preference would be given an individual, for example, not according to Blacks' feelings of solidarity with her but rather to whether or not the majority of the White population—the presumptive wrong-allocators—perceive her to be Black. It would certainly seem a poor remedial system which denied someone an anti-discrimination remedy because she was not felt "Black" by Blacks, if at the same time the rest of the population treated her as if she were.[32]

Other administrative systems have given more attention to developing clear and consistent rules for making such determinations. Yet these particular systems are not ones from which we today are eager to learn. Ford points out: "It would be ironic indeed if for the intelligible administration of modern anti-discrimination law we borrowed our models of procedural rectitude in part from our own segregationist past or from the *apartheid* state of South Africa," but "if we must administer a race-conscious public policy . . . we have to understand that categorization requires method."[33]

Malone v. Haley and the movement to add mixed race to the federal census exemplify two extremely different kinds of pressure on the ethno-racial pentagon. The problem of keeping whites like the Malone brothers from taking unfair advantage of entitlement programs is nested firmly in the political-economic matrix out of which arose the entitlement programs that consolidated the ethno-racial pentagon in the 1970s. Yet the problem of meeting the demand for multiple identity on the part of mixed-race Americans is located instead in a cultural matrix. The people who lobby the Census Bureau for recognition as mixed race have followed the multiculturalist movement's use of the ethno-racial pentagon as a basic guide to cultural identity in the United States. San Francisco residents asked on a street corner how many racial categories should be listed in the census answered as often as not in strictly cultural terms. They took for granted that the reporter's question was about the public recognition of cultures, not about facilitating entitlements for victims of racism.[34]

Thus the routine, public attribution of cultural significance to the blocs of a pentagon originally designed for the purposes of economic and political equality has brought to a point of tragic contradiction two valuable impulses in contemporary America: the impulse to protect historically disadvantaged populations from the effects of past and continuing discrimination, and the impulse to affirm the variety of cultures that now flourish within the United States and that flourish even within individual Americans. Whatever we as a society decide to do with our ethno-racial pentagon, we will do well to remember both the tragic character and the depth of this contradiction. David Harvey has wisely reminded us that a "politics which seeks to eliminate the processes which give rise" to racism may turn out to look very different from a "politics which merely seeks to give full play to differentiated identities once these have arisen."[35]

Just how prescriptively ethnic American society should be is but one of a legion of questions about affiliation that have intensified during the past generation. A prominent characteristic of our era is a preoccupation with affiliation: when the term "we" is invoked, what community is implied? Affiliation has come to the fore in discussions of scientific knowledge, moral values, nationalism, human rights, and the physical health of the earth. In a multitude of discourses, the claims of particular, historically specific communities have been advanced against claims made on behalf of all humankind. The ethno-racial pentagon is a vivid artifact of a sweeping movement from species to ethnos. Within this larger movement in recent and contemporary intellectual history the multiculturalist debates can be addressed most productively, and a postethnic perspective elaborated most clearly.

CHAPTER 3

From Species to Ethnos

Sexual Behavior in the Human Male. Sexual Behavior in the Human Female.[1] The titles imply an inquiry specieswide in scope. The authors were indeed professional zoologists. But the Kinsey reports were based on interviews with a highly particular zoological sample: men and women in mid-twentieth-century North America, overwhelmingly the cultural products of the United States. Deflation of the universalist pretensions of these studies began almost immediately upon the publication of the first of the two volumes in 1948.[2] The Kinsey reports were destined to become artifacts in an animated and enduring discourse not about humankind but about a particular society and its culture. Librarians were obliged to catalogue them in the science section, but at home, individuals found good reasons to shelve these fascinating tomes next to other books that instructed Americans about themselves: David Riesman's *The Lonely Crowd,* Gunnar Myrdal's *American Dilemma,* and Henry Nash Smith's *Virgin Land.* What started out as zoology ended up as a classic of American studies.

Dr. Kinsey and his staff shared with a multitude of their American contemporaries a destiny against which intellectuals of our own time struggle conspicuously. This destiny is to have confused the local with the universal: to have made claims about or claims on behalf of all human-kind for which the salient referent was later said to be but a fragment of that elusive whole. Global perspectives were fashionable in the World War II era, but today we are expert in finding the blind spots in the ostensibly uni-versalist projects of that era. It is a mark of our time how sensitive we have become to the pretensions of a host of these endeavors, once proclaimed with confidence. Con-sider some convenient examples.

In the name of a mystical humanity, the prophetic Hoosier Wendell Willkie, the Republican nominee for presi-dent in 1940, proclaimed *One World.* This extraordinary best-seller of 1943 left the impression that Ukrainian farmers near Kiev deserved our sympathy and respect because they were just like farmers near Kokomo, Indiana.[3] The justification for a global perspective turned out to be that all people were, after all, pretty much alike, a view widely discredited today. In the name of the rights and needs of the entire species, the United States in Willkie's time advanced through war and diplomacy interests that we are now more inclined to bring down to historically particular size: perhaps the interests at issue for Americans in World War II and the cold war were those of the North Atlantic capitalist democracies?

In the name of *The Family of Man,* Edward Steichen and the Museum of Modern Art exhibited a series of photographs that served to remind Americans of the 1950s that men and women from a multitude of foreign and apparently exotic cultures shared their own emotions and experiences.[4] Although this great exhibition, and the book based upon it, no doubt stimulated feelings of human solidarity across many dividing lines, today's celebrants of human diversity are quick to find fault with it. Steichen's pictures of Asians and Africans growing up, marrying, and struggling through their adult lives at work and at home seem to reduce the population of the globe to a set of mirrors for the narrower world of middle-class liberal males of Steichen's milieu. Steichen, like Willkie, achieved a specieswide view by limiting the range and depth of human differences.

In the name of an essential human nature, Freudians and behaviorists offered the entire planet prescriptions that now seem culturally specific. In the name of specieswide fraternity, advocates of Esperanto sought to mitigate the divisive effects of linguistic diversity throughout the world, but this synthetic language was distinctly European. In the name of the epistemological unity of all humankind, philosophers of a positivist orientation vindicated the progress of sciences we are now inclined to situate historically in the most masculine of the intellectual engagements of a distinctive North Atlantic civilization. In the name of a universal capacity for spiritual experience, religious ecumenists aimed to neutralize sectarian conflict through the claim that "we all believe in the same God," who turned out, of course, to be the God of liberal Protestantism.

To resist the extravagant universalism discernible in the scientific, social-scientific, humanistic, religious, and political discourse of the generation represented by the Kinsey reports is to belong to the sprawling cohort I am here calling "we." We history-conscious members of the generation experiencing the end of the century—and of the millennium—realize that Kinsey's generation was far from the first to conflate the local with the universal, but the legacy of this mid-twentieth-century American generation presents a special challenge for us. Not only have our Kinseys and Willkies and Steichens been close at hand; their universalism was often directed against certain particularisms we still take to be evil.

These still-troubling particularisms include white supremacy and other forms of racism and ethnic prejudice. They include, also, nationalist chauvinism, religious bigotry and obscurantism, and a host of provincial taboos. The critical scrutiny of Jim Crow racism in the American South and the search for continuities in the world's religious and mythological systems partook of a common egalitarian impulse; Carey McWilliams's *Brothers under the Skin* and Joseph Campbell's *The Hero with a Thousand Faces* both displayed the faith that a recognition of human similarities was a generous and humane step toward a more just and tolerant world.[5] So, too, was this faith expressed in the United Nations Declaration on Human Rights, promoted by one of the world's leading universalists, Eleanor Roosevelt.

The constraining particularisms fought by the World War II generation also included the several authoritarian warrants for belief associated with the names of T. D. Lysenko and Joseph Goebbels. Lysenko's purge of Soviet genetics in the interests of a politically progressive science and Goebbels's supervision of the Nazi regime's racist cultural programs are, indeed, supreme emblems for the enclosures resisted by American intellectuals of the midcentury decades. These men and women lived in an age when the world was almost conquered by a regime that got away with distinguishing between Aryan physics and Jewish physics, and was almost saved by a regime that distinguished between bourgeois and proletarian science. It was partly to break down these claims of blood and history that these men and women looked to the species as a whole and reasserted Enlightenment notions of knowledge and rights.

Hence one might logically expect that resistance to the

universalist enthusiasms of the midcentury generation would take the form of a yet more rigorous universalism, according to which the covertly particularist biases of our Kinseys and Willkies and Steichens would be eliminated. If that generation confused the local with the universal, let the next generation, with its greater cultural self-awareness, look beyond the local to the genuinely universal. But that is not what has happened. On the contrary, humankind has come to seem too broad a referent. One might say that species-centered discourse has become suspect.

Not everyone has been caught up equally in this flight from the species. Some have sought to refine the old universalism in political contexts, especially in relation to human rights abroad and to civil rights at home. American protests against South Africa's apartheid system were often couched in universalist terms. Some scientists and scholars have represented more critically the fields of experience in which their objects of study can be found, while continuing to strive for insights that can apply to enlarged domains and can be justified by standards recognized in many cultures. The work of the philosopher Thomas Nagel is a prominent example of an attempt to defend epistemic universalism while displaying genuine sensitivity to the diversity and particularity of human inquirers.[6]

But alongside these efforts to serve universalist ideals there have appeared during the past several decades a multitude of initiatives of a very different sort. *Retribal-*

ization was the word suggested for this trend by one of the first observers to comment on it within and beyond American society, Harold R. Isaacs.[7] The early 1970s, when Isaacs wrote, is the chronological point at which the contrast between an older species-consciousness and a newer ethnic-consciousness can be seen most vividly. It was then that Erik Erikson popularized his concept of "pseudospeciation," responding to what he perceived as the inability of many people to achieve healthy psychological identities with large human collectivities. One of Erikson's most pointed discussions of pseudospeciation took place in the course of an exchange about black nationalism with the Black Panther leader Huey Newton.[8]

At virtually the same moment Isaacs and Erikson wrote, Jacob Bronowski, a resolute defender of the older universalism, produced an ambitious popular book in connection to a thirteen-part series of programs for public television. *The Ascent of Man*[9] might have done very well if it had appeared fifteen or twenty years earlier, in the era of Steichen's *Family of Man*. Bronowski's vigorously species-centered account of the progressive steps taken by human beings, most often through the activities of male inventors and scientists, was soon all but forgotten. The unself-conscious masculinity of Bronowski's sense of the species and its history renders *The Ascent of Man* an especially poignant example of a mode of thought that was placed sharply on the defensive immediately after Bronowski wrote.

In our own time, we find new pride in our sense of historical particularity. The science we believe and practice derives its validity, we are sometimes told, not from its presumed capacity for verification across the lines of all the world's cultures but from the authority of the distinctive social entities Thomas S. Kuhn and his followers have helped us to recognize: sharply bounded professional communities characterized by rigorous procedures for the acculturation of their members. The obligations we owe to one another and the rights we claim for ourselves derive not from our common membership in a species; our new moral philosophers tell us that these obligations and rights derive from the ordinance of the traditions of our own tribe.

Thus we are told that the universalism of the World War II era served to deracinate and to efface the varieties of humankind by using a too parochial construction of our common humanity; further, we are told that this universalism served to mask a cultural imperialism by which the NATO powers spread throughout the world their own peculiar standards for truth, justice, and spiritual perfection. If these claims are true, we are told, then universalism itself is too dangerous an ideal. Let us emphasize instead the integrity of all the varieties of humankind, let us encourage every culture to find its own distinctive voice, let us enable the repressed other to command our attention through new canons and curricula, and thereby to destroy the cultural hierarchy created by Western prejudice. So, we beat the drums for "alterity"—a popular new word for "the other"—and wonder whether the defense of Salman Rushdie's freedom of speech is not another bourgeois conceit, the salient functions of which are to prevent Muslims from worshiping in peace and to enable Western intellectuals to feel superior to the still benighted East.

Hence the covert enthnocentrism we now discern within the species-centered discourse of the World War II generation has come to stand not as an invitation to develop a yet more rigorous universalism but rather as proof of the impossibility of escaping ethnocentrism. Our mission, apparently, is not to purge the old universalism of its corruptions but to renounce it as fatally flawed and to perfect instead the local and the particular, to live within the confines of the unique civic, moral, and epistemic communities into which we are born, to devote ourselves to our ethnos.

We are humble in the face of the mistakes we know our predecessors have made in the name of the species. How many ideas, once solemnly and confidently taken to be warranted by our best science, are now discredited and often explained historically by the racist and sexist biases of scientific communities? How many injustices have been committed by people who believed they were acting on the basis of scientific truth? How many "feeble-minded" women were sterilized by Virginia public-health physicians acting on this precious authority?[10] Do not such cases show the wisdom of Michel Foucault's observation that "knowledge is not made for understanding; it is made for cutting"?[11] The authority of knowledge celebrated by the Enlightenment can be a dangerous thing. We are quick to acknowledge the historically situated character of our own judgments. The growing acceptance since the 1960s and 1970s of our own historicity has much to do with the transition from species to ethnos.

By *historicity* I mean simply the contingent, temporally, and socially situated character of our beliefs and values, of our institutions and practices.[12] When we accept our own historical particularity, we shy away from essentialist constructions of human nature, from transcendentalist arguments about it, and from timeless rules for justifying claims about it. We eschew the Archimedean perspective, and we instead inquire outward from our experience. We practice immanent rather than transcendental critique. We confront the insight that truths and rights and obligations become available to us—and thus, it is apparently easy to conclude, come into existence for us—through the operation of historically specific communities of human beings.

Antecedents of this historicism are easy to find, in nineteenth-century German hermeneutics, for example, in the turn-of-the-century American pragmatists, and in the cultural relativism associated with the anthropologists led by Franz Boas. But one work of the post-1945 era that commandingly represents this new historicist movement is of course Kuhn's 1962 classic, *The Structure of Scientific Revolutions*.[13] This book was addressed to science, and specifically to the most mathematically developed and technical of the sciences; however, its apparent demonstration of the dependence of scientific truth on the historically specific practice of distinctively organized human communities gave unprecedented credibility to the historicist perspective as applied elsewhere. If even the most persuasively verified claims of astronomers and physicists were to a significant extent cultural products, what could be said about the claims of social scientists and humanistic scholars, of moral philosophers, metaphysicians, and political theorists, and others whose ability to get beyond opinion and prejudice had always been precarious and contested?

There were still distinctions to be made, of course: one could posit a spectrum of claims running from the relative universality of warrant to the relative locality of warrant, with the periodic table of elements at one end and the value of a good sun tan at the other. But in the wake of the transformation for which Kuhn's name has become an emblem, this whole spectrum shifted toward the local. It thus became more plausible to view the Bill of Rights as just another tribal code than as a manifestation in one polity of claims advanced on behalf of all humankind. This rather anthropological way of looking at our own culture was resoundingly proclaimed by Clifford Geertz, whose fieldwork in Indonesia and Morocco made him the era's most influential anthropologist. Geertz urged that we should see "ourselves amongst others, as a local example of the forms human life has locally taken, a case among cases, a world among worlds."[14] Eric R. Wolf may have been right to remind us that "a common destiny" unites "the peoples who have asserted a privileged relation with history and the peoples to whom history has been denied," but can our knowledge of that "common destiny" be anything other than "local"?[15]

Even Geertz's localism came to seem relatively solicitous of global perspectives when a movement of younger anthropologists, even more determined than Geertz to renounce the epistemic arrogance associated with European colonialism, put more and more of their energies into telling their own stories rather than studying distant societies and cultures.[16] One, having produced a distinguished study of headhunters in the Philippines, wrote about his own experiences in the field and about their apparent epistemological significance and turned to ethnographical investigations within his own ethnic group near his own university.[17] Another, having written two successful books about the people of Nepal, undertook an ethnographic study of her own high school class in New Jersey.[18] Although these new directions of anthropological work have produced some valuable results, the sites of anthropological creativity do appear to be changing.

By the 1980s even the great Kantian philosopher John Rawls had sidled cautiously toward the historicists, locating the process of reasoning toward justice in a more socially dense and particular setting than he had in his earlier work.[19] Rawls's drift toward the ethnos left academic leadership of the resistance in the hands of dwindling cadres of Jesuits and of the followers of Leo Strauss, the émigré philosopher whose defense of natural law won a devoted, if small, constituency in American academia. And if historicists of the Kuhn-Geertz variety fell forward on their faces as the positivist opposition they had always pressed against virtually collapsed in many of the traditional arenas of struggle, they were run over from behind by the poststructuralists, for whom the very impulse to produce all-encompassing theories and narratives was a mistake, a temptation to be overcome.

Whatever else poststructuralism has contributed, it has helped to constitute the more general phenomenon known as postmodernism. Some formulations of the touted transition from modernism to postmodernism run roughly parallel to the transition from species-centered discourse to ethnos-centered discourse. Modernism and postmodernism are of course highly contested terms, conveying a number of different meanings in the contemporary debate, but postmodernist doctrine is frequently invoked to condemn the Enlightenment project and to confer attention and dignity on the local, the fragmentary, and the particular. Amid the welter of constructions and counterconstructions of the modern and the postmodern, the species is very often to the modern what the ethnos is to the postmodern. This ethnicization of all discourse through the decentering strategies of postmodernism is thus a culmination of the process by which the term *ethnic* has lost its connotations of marginality. Originally, ethnic meant "outsider," "pagan," or "gentile,"[20] but it has come to stand for situatedness within virtually any bounded community, regardless of its relation to other communities.

Meanwhile, a chorus of both academic and popular political voices identified ethno-racial communities as vital sites for the formation, articulation, and sustenance of cultural values, social identities, and political power. Texts once celebrated for their apparent ability to speak to and for all people came to be valued as representatives of distinct social constituencies defined largely by the author's ethno-racial identity and gender. *Diversity* replaced *unity* in the slogans of those concerned to promote mutual respect and equality among the varieties of humankind found within the United States. The once-popular notion that there might be an American character or even culture was widely discredited as a nationalist equivalent of a universalism understood to deny diversity. The ethnos came to be defined in opposition not only to the species but also to the closest thing to its national equivalent, the American nation. The figure of the melting pot, encumbered with assimilationist connotations, lost favor to the salad bowl, the mosaic, and the garden of plants each with its own autochthonous roots. The United States came increasingly to be represented as a complex patchwork of distinctive communities, sometimes said to be nationlike, each one a unique product of distinctive historical forces and circumstances. An ideological and constitutional tradition protecting the rights of individuals was asked to reform itself in order to protect instead the rights of groups.

The phenomena we have come to call multiculturalism thus partake of a larger transition from species to ethnos in the recent intellectual history of the United States. While some commentaries on multiculturalism present it as simply an outgrowth of the political and cultural affirmations of American minority groups since the 1960s, multiculturalism is more than that. Gerald Early puts the point too strongly when he insists that both the origins and the "premises" of multiculturalism are to be found in postmodernism's attack on "the bourgeois intellectual order as inherently political and interested," but he is correct to see these two movements as frequently overlapping and drawing strength from each other.[21]

The transition from species to ethnos is an event that transcends the United States, which can be construed as one of many national sites for its production. Within the United States it has been the most visible in the social-scientific and humanistic sections of higher education and in the literary life beyond the academy. It has been the least visible among Americans of a more conservative political or religious orientation.

The scale of this event in recent American intellectual history is difficult to measure. No doubt it is easy to exaggerate the intensity, scope, and singularity of the historicist and particularist enthusiasms of the last three decades and to likewise exaggerate the strength and unity of universalist initiatives of the previous era. But if the decline of species-centered discourse and the enlargement of ethnos-centered discourse does not affect everyone, it affects a sufficient segment of educated Americans to demand historical notice and critical assessment. Rather than speculate about what, in the dynamics of the postwar period, might be the several causes of this change in the center of intellectual gravity for many Americans, I want simply to call attention to it and to observe that this transformation has served to greatly increase the importance of issues in *affiliation*.

The importance of affiliation can be seen in the new prominence of the notion of community in discussions of truths, meanings, rights, and goods. In the post-Kuhnian era, argumentation about knowledge is, much more than it used to be, argumentation about epistemic communities. Exactly who gets to decide what ideas are counted as true?

Stanley Fish, treating communities of readers as analogues to Kuhn's communities of scientists, proposed that the meaning of texts was a matter decided by a profession of literary critics, who also decided what was and was not a "text" to begin with.[22] Political theorist Michael Walzer organized his "radically particularist" *Spheres of Justice* around the issue of membership in a "community." In working out his analysis, Walzer explicitly eschewed any effort to look outside the Platonic cave of his own tribe.[23] Richard Rorty, addressing both epistemic and moral communities, argued that communal "solidarity" can perform the services for which people once turned naively to the ideal of "objectivity."

Rorty, in an exchange with Geertz, sketched a pluralist vision of the world as an expanse of private, exclusive clubs, interacting with as much civility as they could, but each defined, animated, and sustained by a vivid sense of the difference between "we" and "they." When it comes to justifying a truth claim, whom do we have to persuade? Whose testimony do we need to take into account? Why, the members of our own club, of our own epistemic community. When it comes to justifying rights and obligations, whom do we have to persuade? Whose opinions and sensibilities do we need to take into account? Why, the members of our own club, our own moral community. Rorty even suggested that "the exclusivity of the private club might be a crucial feature of an ideal world order."[24] Geertz himself did not go that far, but he agreed that "community" was "the shop in which thoughts are constructed and deconstructed," and that "history" was the "terrain they seize and surrender."[25]

Along with the new prominence of community comes a new centrality for the old question of membership: The less one's raw humanity is said to count for anything, the more important one's affiliations become. The more epistemic and moral authority is ascribed to historically particular communities, the more it does matter just who is and is not one of "us." The more detached truth and goodness become from the testimony and tastes of any population outside our own tribe or club, the more is at stake when that tribe or club defines itself in relation to other human beings. How wide the circle of the "we"?

This may be *the* great question in an age of ethnos-centered discourse. The frequency with which it is asked with some urgency, even by such sophisticated discussants as the philosopher Bernard Williams, helps to distinguish our own, historical moment.[26] The centrality of this question to academic debates is matched by its centrality to public policy in an era when illegal immigration and a multitude of political refugees from Cuba, Haiti, and elsewhere force the issue in the halls of government. What do "we" owe to refugees, and what gives "them" any claim they have on "us"?

Many old, nonhistoricist questions within academic debate translate into the terms of this newly prominent question of the "we." Consider, for example, two old chestnuts especially favored by intellectuals of the 1930s and 1940s, subjectivity versus objectivity and relativism versus absolutism. Subjectivity was most often depicted, in those years, as an individual, psychological state, and objectivity as access to the domain of the external world. Can history be objective, can ethics be objective, is science really objective? these intellectuals asked, while contrasting the values and preconceptions of the individual subject to an objective reality. What has happened since then is a collectivization of the subjective. It has become a population of minds who get their capacity to think as they do from a paradigm, an episteme, or a code, or some other structure that exists prior to the individual mind being shaped by it. To be sure, subjectivity was sometimes back then—fifty or sixty years ago—defined in terms of deference to tribal norms rather than in terms of individual idiosyncrasy, but the trend is unmistakable. Peter Novick has caught the difference in his recent study of the objectivity question among professional historians, noting the transition in relativism from Carl Becker's "Everyman His Own Historian" in 1932 to "Every Group Its Own Historian" since the 1960s.[27]

In the meantime, within the swelling ranks of the historicists, those counted as defenders of objectivity (now usually in quotation marks) turn out to be defenders of large-scale consensus. An example is Kuhn, who has formulated his disagreement with Rorty by purposefully conflating objectivity with Rorty's ideal of solidarity: "Like solidarity, objectivity extends only over the world of the tribe, but what it extends over is no less firm and real for that," Kuhn insisted. But Kuhn's tribe is large—Kuhn says he can imagine no life without the "single character" for which he takes both "objectivity" and "solidarity" to be names—while Rorty's club is small.[28]

Or, so it once was. Rorty was an adamant defender of ethnocentrism in the mid-1980s, but by the 1990s he was developing a more and more inclusive notion of the ethnos of which he took himself and his readers to be part. Rorty's own changes in emphasis are worth tracing and analyzing here because the recent career of this philosopher—one of the most prolific and widely discussed American thinkers of our time—registers with rare cogency many of the most important opportunities and dilemmas of ethnos-centered discourse. His attraction to ethnocentrism and his gradual withdrawal from it offer a striking case study.

In the mid-1980s, when Rorty first began to call by the name of ethnocentrism his insistence that we need not orient ourselves to the species, Rorty stressed how limited was the interchange he envisioned between the various clans that divide people from one another, and how lacking all such clans were in obligations to one another's members. In one of his most evocative discussions of the problem, Rorty took up the hypothetical case of "a child found wandering in the woods, the remnant of a slaughtered nation whose temples have been razed and whose books have been burned." Such a lost child is said to have, on Rorty's radically historicist principles, no claim to "human dignity" because the moral community that sustained this notion in his or her case no longer exists. True, says Rorty, but if the lost child is fortunate enough to be found by "us," by representatives of our ethnos, we will take the child into our community, there "to be reclothed with dignity." Why? Because this child is indeed human, and our ethnos carries the universalist aspirations of the Judeo-Christian tradition, "gratefully invoked," says Rorty candidly, "by free-loading atheists like myself."[29]

Even in Rorty's view, it is membership in our species that endows the lost child with human dignity, but only because this biological and species-ist basis for dignity happens to be recognized by our particular Western ethnos. Does this make our culture superior to others? Only in our eyes, it would seem. But when our eyes are directed at "our own," we do, according to Rorty, have special responsibilities. It is in discussing these responsibilities in contemporary America that Rorty made his strongest, yet his most pragmatic, witness against the old universalism:

> Consider . . . the attitude of contemporary American liberals to the unending hopelessness and misery of the lives of young blacks in American cities. Do we

say that these people must be helped because they are our fellow human beings? We may, but it is much more persuasive, morally as well as politically, to describe them as our fellow *Americans*—to insist that it is outrageous than an *American* should live without hope. . . . [O]ur sense of solidarity is strongest when those with whom solidarity is expressed are thought of as "one of us," where "us" means something smaller and more local than the human race.[30]

Here, Rorty drew the ethnocentric circle to correspond with American citizenship. He did so for a specific and admirable purpose: he hopes that some humans might be more effectively inspired to act to diminish the suffering of others. Yet the suffering Rorty wants to diminish has been created and perpetuated by the feeling among many white Americans that blacks are not really part of "us" anyway. Distinctions between Americans of different racial and ethnic groups yield formidable we-they dynamics of their own. Indeed, such dynamics gave rise in the first place to the concept of ethnocentrism, which Rorty now wishes to appropriate for two benign purposes: to flag the recognition of our own historical particularity and to inspire, Rorty hopes, a measure of generosity greater than that previously called forth by appeals to the common humanity of all sufferers.

That such appeals to a grand humanity have failed to prevent a multitude of cruelties is easy to demonstrate, but Rorty has been less concerned to measure the practical efficacy of these old universalist appeals than to warn against the Kantian rationalism with which he persistently associates them. Kant made morality a matter of rational deduction from general principles, Rorty complains, and made "feelings of pity and benevolence ... seem dubious, second-rate motives for not being cruel." But these motives are altogether praiseworthy, according to Rorty, who spent much of his 1989 book, *Contingency, Irony, and Solidarity,* arguing that novelists, ethnographers, essayists, and other "nonphilosophical" intellectuals can do a lot more for the cause of human solidarity than can the Kantian thinkers who try to identify a "human essence" and to establish a "rational obligation" in relation to it. Rorty's ethnocentrism is directed more sharply against rationalist and essentialist constructions of human nature than against any appeals to the solidarity of a historically real population. The extremity of Rorty's ethnocentrism was revealed by the end of the 1980s to be a disagreement with other philosophers over the terms on which human solidarity should be affirmed. As soon as the Kantians are disposed of, Rorty's vision of human solidarity takes on a decidedly anti-ethnocentric cast: this solidarity, says Rorty, should be understood as "the ability to think of people wildly different from ourselves as included in the range of 'us'."[31]

Hence it is fair to observe that Rorty wants to mobilize all the liberal, cosmopolitan instincts that have been directed against ethnocentrism by John Dewey, Franz

Boas, Ruth Benedict, and their kind, but Rorty is so fearful of universalist claims that he takes pains to characterize this venerable anti-ethnocentrism as a tribal peculiarity of ours, and thus as part of the ethnos about which Rorty proposes to be ethnocentric. Rorty may assure us that the circle of the we can never be expected to embrace all humankind, but he manages to put in place a particularist cover for chastened gestures toward universalism. By the end of the 1980s Rorty was ready to allow that it would be fine to try to "extend our sense of 'we' to people whom we have previously thought of as 'they'." On the final page of *Contingency, Irony, and Solidarity,* he decisively extended the circle of the "we": what we must build, he now declared, is "an ever larger and more variegated *ethnos,*" for a crucial feature of our ethnos is, after all, its traditional "distrust" of "ethnocentrism."[32]

By 1993 Rorty was calling for the creation of a "planetary community" defined by "human rights." The great question for Rorty remained how to diminish human suffering, and he was more convinced than ever that it would do no good to hold forth on metaphysical principles about human nature and about the moral obligation rational creatures owed to one another. What was needed, according to Rorty, was the spread of a "human rights culture." This goal was more likely to be achieved by "sentimental education" than by "moral knowledge," and it was rendered more realistic by an economic security the absence of which was the chief obstacle to the spread of species-consciousness. Rorty's program was intended not to bolster each clan's feeling of distinctive solidarity within but to break down the hatred for others sustained by such solidarities: we are to try to "expand the reference of the terms *our sort of people* and *people like us*."[33]

The most salient features of Rorty's position in 1993 were his fierce attack on tribalism, his uninhibited embrace of all humankind as the potential beneficiary of the human rights culture derived from Christianity and the Enlightenment, and his uncompromising willingness to defend human rights against the claims of cultures that failed to support these rights. Even Rorty, then, has come around to insisting that full recognition of the historically particular character of our discourses should not be taken as a license for abandoning a traditional human rights commitment, nor for what Geertz lampooned as "parochialism without tears,"[34] the giving up on the venerable cosmopolitan project of looking sympathetically beyond one's immediate surroundings. Rorty, as a defender of human rights, had managed by 1993 to distance himself dramatically from a syndrome criticized by the Aristotelian philosopher Martha Nussbaum on the basis of her experience at a series of international conferences concerned with the welfare of people in developing countries.

Nussbaum heard anthropologists attack "Western essentialist medicine" for its "binary oppositions" such as life and death, and health and disease. One lamented the introduction of smallpox vaccination to India by the British because it "eradicated the cult of Sittala Devi, the goddess to whom one used to pray in order to avert smallpox," and thus exemplified "Western neglect of difference." The pained Nussbaum observed:

> Highly intelligent people, people deeply committed to the good of women and men in developing countries, people who think of themselves as progressive and feminist and antiracist, are taking up positions that converge . . . with the positions of reaction, oppression, and sexism. Under the banner of their radical and politically correct "antiessentialism" march ancient religious taboos . . . ill health, ignorance, and death.[35]

Rorty remains an anti-essentialist, but he no longer attacks essentialism in terms that promote the syndrome Nussbaum identified. Rorty's effort to detach the concept of ethnocentrism from its conventional meaning has succeeded chiefly as a sophisticated irony, challenging people with lingering universalist tendencies to recognize the historical particularity of their own anti-ethnocentrism. But even if ethnocentrism has served Rorty poorly, the dead ends and contradictions displayed by his forthright, admirably risk-taking deployment of this concept against the conceits of his colleagues are highly instructive. These dead ends and contradictions can help to inspire a posteth-nic disposition toward issues of affiliation in a variety of contexts. One context in which these terms are now debated with great earnestness is the discussion over the destiny of the American civic community. Indeed, nowhere is ethnos-centered discourse more apparent than in these multiculturalist debates.

CHAPTER 4

Pluralism, Cosmopolitanism, and the Diversification of Diversity

That the United States ought to be home to a number of distinctive cultures, especially those associated with different ethno-racial affiliations, is now widely accepted. But the implications of this basic multiculturalist idea remain decidedly unresolved. Does the United States have an ethnos of its own, or is the nation best seen as a container of cultures defined largely by ethno-racial communities? How autonomous and how enduring are the communities credited with producing America's many cultures? Are all of these cultures of equal value and demanding of equal attention in education? What relation do these ethno-racially based cultures have with cultures that are not derived from ethno-racial communities? What hopes can we have that projects in cultural reform can diminish political and economic inequalities? To what extent can an emphasis on the differences between people promote the goal of human equality?

These questions, over which multiculturalists disagree among themselves, have been too often obscured by the prevailing terms of the great multiculturalist debate of the last several years. Participants in these debates frequently characterize each other as separatists or as defenders of Eurocentric domination; they often construct the issues as a series of choices between similarity or difference, wholeness or fragmentation, assimilation or dissimilation, and uniformity or diversity. No doubt these terms describe fairly some participants in this debate and some of the doctrines advanced. But these terms more often amount to opprobrious epithets. The debate is too often scripted as a two-sided confrontation between traditionalists who want a uniform culture grounded in "Western Civilization" as presented by colleges in the 1950s and progressives who appreciate difference and promote diversity. Defenders of multiculturalism have complained with good reason that critics have lumped together indiscriminately a range of distinctive ideas offered in the name of multiculturalism, but the next step is all too often to return the favor by sweeping all critics of multiculturalism into a single army of reactionaries.[1] Part of the problem is that virtually no one defends monoculturalism,[2] with the result that multiculturalism is deprived of an honest, natural opposite.

Eurocentrism is often said to be multiculturalism's most immediate and active enemy, but this concept, like monoculturalism, is more a polemicist's device than a fair description of any but a few of the people who have worried aloud about the cultural fragmentation of the United States and a loss of pedagogic focus in the nation's classrooms.[3] And many who do uphold European traditions insist that what makes these traditions worth defending is their multitudinous, decidedly multicultural character.[4] Hence the "opponents" of multiculturalism sometimes end up claiming its banner as their own, while a more-multiculturalist-than-thou faction simultaneously complains that a merely cosmetic acceptance of multiculturalism masks a conservative victory in the culture wars and a rejection of "true" multiculturalism.

Henry Louis Gates, Jr., defends what he calls multiculturalism in the midst of an incisive attack on what many critics of multiculturalism take to be its most salient expression, identity politics.[5] Diane Ravitch is often treated as an enemy of multiculturalism because of her criticisms of particularism, especially as manifest in Afrocentrist curricula, but Ravitch has repeatedly declared herself to be in favor of multiculturalism.[6] One of the world's leading exponents of traditional liberal philosophy, Joseph Raz, has fashioned multiculturalism as a liberal initiative, while it has been developed as a critical initiative by a Chicago collective skeptical in the extreme of traditional liberal strategies.[7] The widespread triumph of the basic multiculturalist idea and the shrewd determination of most discussants to claim the multiculturalist label for themselves has rendered the word "multiculturalism" a shibboleth. Behind this shibboleth are concealed a variety of persuasions and counterpersuasions well worth drawing out into the open in the interests of addressing in a more forthright manner the issues that have given rise to the multiculturalist debate to begin with.

To this purpose, one can look more closely at a single example, a recent essay by the 1994–95 president of the Organization of American Historians, Gary B. Nash of UCLA. Nash defends multiculturalism, which he takes to be an emphasis on diversity, an elimination of ethnocentrism, and the "integration of the histories of both genders and people of all classes and racial or ethnic groups."[8] Indeed, Nash is the principal author of a widely discussed series of textbooks recently adopted by most public school districts in California and designed explicitly to serve these multiculturalist goals.[9] Yet Nash is insistently critical of the Afrocentrism that is sometimes counted as a version of multiculturalism. Nash finds fault with the ethnocentric reasoning by which our schools might be asked to design "Sinocentrist," "Khmercentrist," and "Hispanocentrist" curricula, and to ignore the needs of "mixed-race children in a society where . . . interracial marriage is at an all-time high." Nash defends the idea of "common ground" in terms that might well have come from multiculturalism's critics. "If multiculturalism is to get beyond a promiscuous pluralism that gives everything equal weight and adopts complete moral relativism," says Nash, "it must reach some agreement on what is at the core of American culture."[10]

Moreover, Nash is very direct in telling us what we should take as that core: the democratic values "clearly stated" in the nation's "founding documents." These old principles "are a precious heritage" endowing with the same rights all "individuals" of "whatever group attachments." Nash thus alludes to the nation's nonethnic ideological tradition and points to that tradition's helpful role in "virtually every social and political struggle carried out by women, religious minorities, labor, and people of color." Scorning the varieties of particularism that encourage young people to identify only with antecedents of their own ethno-racial category, Nash insists that "Harriet Tubman and Ida B. Wells should inspire all students, not simply African-American females." He further reminds us that W. E. B. Du Bois once "wed" a color-neutral "Truth" and sought to "live above the veil" of color by learning from Aristotle and Shakespeare. Nash several times invokes "cosmopolitanism," a concept that matches his ideas more comfortably than does the more ambiguous "multiculturalism" with which he, like so many other opponents of a narrowly Anglo-Protestant curriculum and public culture, finds himself saddled.[11]

Sharpening the distinction between cosmopolitanism and some of the other persuasions that reside in and around multiculturalism may help to clarify the issues. The word *cosmopolitanism* has sometimes been used as a synonym for *universalism*, on the basis of the correct understanding that cosmopolitans look beyond a province or nation to the larger sphere of humankind that is the object of universalists. Both terms can be comfortably applied to many statements made in the species-centered discourse of the era of World War II. Yet these two words can serve us best if we use them not as synonyms but as labels for significantly different orientations toward the wider world to which both are attentive.

We can distinguish a universalist will to find common ground from a cosmopolitan will to engage human diversity. Cosmopolitanism shares with all varieties of universalism a profound suspicion of enclosures, but cosmopolitanism is defined by an additional element not essential to universalism itself: recognition, acceptance, and eager exploration of diversity. Cosmopolitanism urges each individual and collective unit to absorb as much varied experience as it can, while retaining its capacity to advance its aims effectively. For cosmopolitans, the diversity of humankind is a fact; for universalists, it is a potential problem. Hence multiculturalists have reason to find diversity-appreciating cosmopolitanism much less suspect than unity-seeking universalism.

But an additional distinction is even more vital to the task of breaking the logjams of the multiculturalist debates. A tension between cosmopolitanism and pluralism runs throughout these debates, is rarely acknowledged, and is increasingly acute as resistance to essential multiculturalism diminishes. That the concept of multiculturalism was amorphous mattered little when its adherents were fewer and when alliances had to be made against people who were slow to appreciate the need for it. Pluralism and cosmopolitanism have often been united in the common cause of promoting tolerance and diversity. Hence they have not always been distinguished as sharply as I believe today's circumstances demand. But now that so many parties are claiming multiculturalism as their own, the issues within multiculturalism should receive more open and extended discussion. Many of these issues fall into view once the pluralist–cosmopolitan distinction is developed and confronted.

Pluralism differs from cosmopolitanism in the degree to which it endows with privilege particular groups, especially the communities that are well established at whatever time the ideal of pluralism is invoked. While cosmopolitanism is willing to put the future of every culture at risk through the sympathetic but critical scrutiny of other cultures, pluralism is more concerned to protect and perpetuate particular, existing cultures. In its extreme form, this conservative concern takes the form of a bargain: "You keep the acids of your modernity out of my culture, and I'll keep the acids of mine away from yours." If cosmopolitanism can be casual about community building and community maintenance and tends to seek voluntary affiliations of wide compass, pluralism promotes affiliations on the narrower grounds of shared history and is more quick to see reasons for drawing boundaries between communities.

Cosmopolitanism is more oriented to the individual, whom it is likely to understand as a member of a number of different communities simultaneously. Pluralism is more oriented to the group, and is likely to identify each individual with reference to a single, primary community. Cosmopolitanism is more suspicious than is pluralism of the potential for conformist pressures within the communities celebrated by pluralists, while pluralism is more suspicious than is cosmopolitanism of the variousness and lack of apparent structure in the wider world celebrated by cosmopolitans. Arguments offered by universalists that certain interests are shared by many, if not all, groups will get a longer hearing from cosmopolitans than from pluralists. The latter are more likely to see in such arguments the covert advancement of the interests of one particular group.

This tension between pluralism and cosmopolitanism is not novel to the multiculturalist debates. In less acute form it can be found throughout the long history of discourse about the character of diversity in the United States.[12] By attending briefly to that history, we can better understand the ways in which multiculturalism is a continuation of an old conversation, and the ways in which it is a highly distinctive episode.

The national motto, *E Pluribus Unum,* displayed from the republic's start a sense that whatever singularity the nation achieved was to be constructed out of diverse materials. This appreciation for multiplicity derived in large part from the fact that thirteen different sovereignties needed to be incorporated into a single political authority. But it derived also from the new nation's social and religious heterogeneity, especially as lived and sometimes celebrated in the colonial past of polyglot Pennsylvania and New York. The notion that the United States was the vehicle for the development of a new, amalgamated people was advanced as early as the Revolutionary era in J. Hector St. John de Crèvecoeur's famous praise for the "strange mixture of blood" that made "this new man," the "American." Crèvecoeur's ideal is not quite pluralist, because he does not explicitly envision a series of enduring groups, nor is it unambiguously cosmopolitan. He emphasizes the diversity not of the final product but only of the materials going into it.

What is true of Crèvecoeur is also true of Ralph Waldo Emerson. A generation after Crèvecoeur, Emerson hailed this "asylum of all nations," drawing "the energy of Irish, Germans, Swedes, Poles, and Cossacks, and all the European tribes—of the Africans, and the Polynesians," creating in the process a "new race" as "vigorous as the new Europe which came out of the smelting pot of the Dark Ages."[13] The same emphasis on diversity of base but singleness of product can be found in the most eloquent of all the voices in this tradition, Herman Melville:

We are not a nation, so much as a world. . . . Our
ancestry is lost in the Universal paternity; and Caesar
and Alfred, St. Paul and Luther, and Homer and
Shakespeare are as much ours as Washington. . . .
We are the heirs of all time, and with all nations we
divide our inheritance. On this Western Hemisphere
all tribes and peoples are forming into one federated
whole; and there is a future which shall see the
estranged children of Adam restored as to the old
hearthstone in Eden.[14]

Not everyone shared this appreciation for diversity, which
was always under pressure from what we today would call an
ethnic sense of American nationality, based on the presumed
centrality of British stock.[15] Hence if Melville's peroration
begs the question of how great and how persistent would be
the range of internal differences within the new American
society, once built, Melville was decisively on the side of
diversity where it most counted: in the fight against a narrowly ethnic nationalism and against the idea that some
Americans were more American than others. To "forever
extinguish the prejudices of national dislikes" was what he
took to be the reasonable outcome of sober reflection on "the
mode in which America has been settled."[16]

By virtue of his position in this quarrel against nativists,
Melville is sometimes called a cosmopolitan. In Melville's
own time, however, cosmopolitanism carried implications
of superficiality and even shiftlessness that are altogether

alien to these passages in *Redburn*. Melville was a strong nationalist, while the cosmopolite or cosmopolitan in mid-nineteenth-century America was a well-traveled character probably lacking in substance.[17]

But neither those who sought to circumscribe diversity nor those, like Melville, who sought to expand it bequeathed to the twentieth century any carefully elaborated theory of pluralism or of cosmopolitanism. What they left, instead, was a set of ambiguities that created openings, invited contentions, and fostered confusions that affected the shape and character of twentieth-century efforts to defend diversity, right down to the present day.

One of these inherited ambiguities was at the heart of the very idea of a pluralistic society. Just what human properties served to distinguish people from one another, and thereby to define the many *(pluribus)* to be incorporated into one *(unum)*? Was religious affiliation the salient property? Or was it language, biological ancestry, prior nationality, geographic locality, political ideology, economic interest, or perhaps all of the above? Some references to plurality even in the eighteenth and nineteenth centuries took for granted that the relevant distinctions were those then called racial or national, distinguishing Germans, English, Swedes, Irish, and so forth from one another. But other references to plurality invoked religious denominations, political factions, states of the union, and property interests. That an appropriate form of pluralism was cultural, and that cultural meant what we have since come to call ethnic or perhaps even racial, was far from an established understanding when the twentieth century began.

A second ambiguity had to do with the scope of diversity, even when discussants assumed that ethno-racial distinctions were the stuff of which diversity was made. Did that multiplicity embrace persons of all ethno-racial groups? In practice, the obvious answer to this question was no. The privileged status of British and later of Western European and still later of any European ancestry is now one of the most widely recognized themes in the history of the United States. Several cultural pluralists of the early twentieth century considered themselves radical for appreciating the cultural contributions of Jews, Irish Catholics, and various Slavic and Mediterranean peoples, yet were slow to conceive of the possibility that pluralism might provide legitimacy to peoples known today as African American, Asian American, indigenous, and Latino. But in theory, diversity meant something less restrictive. The privileged status of certain stocks was informal in character, thereby inviting contest by an ever expanding number of marginalized groups in the name of the Enlightenment abstractions implanted in the nation's political charters.

Yet a third ambiguity lay in the extent to which ethno-racial identity implied affiliation with an autonomous and enduring social community. American political ideology and constitutional doctrine so emphasized individuality that the pluralists of the early twentieth century were endowed with very few tools for talking about the claims of groups. The notion of legally protected territorial enclaves for nationality groups was rejected by Congress—first for Irish immigrants in Ohio in 1818, and thirty years later for German immigrants in Texas—but informal clustering and a measure of legally sanctioned residential segregation were obvious facts of American demographic life. It was possible to construe ethno-racial groups as internally coherent subsocieties expected to perpetuate themselves and to attain some measure of recognition as groups. Yet it was more common to regard these groups as fluid, contributing to American diversity by serving as temporary homes for individuals whose descendants would eventually assimilate.

Uncertainty about the character of ethno-racial groups and their place in the larger American society was displayed even in constructions of the melting pot. As it was first construed in the early twentieth century, the melting pot—a figure of speech introduced into the American lexicon by Israel Zangwill's 1908 play of the same name—served to transform not only the immigrants, but everyone, including Mayflower descendants, who were to be improved through a dynamic mixing with immigrants. This notion of "melting" was consistent with the ideas Crèvecoeur, Emerson, and Melville had articulated much earlier. Yet in Zangwill's time this figure of speech also became associated with an antithetical, conformist impulse to melt down the peculiarities of immigrants in order to pour the resulting liquid into pre-existing molds created in the self-image of the Anglo-Protestants who claimed prior possession of America. The significance of ethno-racial groups for American society was radically unresolved when taken up shortly after Zangwill wrote by the men and women who would eventually be remembered as cultural pluralists.

Chief among these was the philosopher Horace Kallen, who in magazine articles published as early as 1915 set forth the ideas that in 1924 he named "cultural pluralism."[18] Kallen envisioned the life of the United States as analogous to a symphony orchestra: each instrument was a distinctive group transplanted from the Old World, making harmonious music with other groups. He emphasized the integrity and autonomy of each descent-defined group. But Kallen's cultural pluralism was defined less sharply as a positive program than as a negative reaction to conformist versions of the melting pot. The massive immigration from eastern and southern Europe since the 1880s had generated an increasingly hostile movement to Americanize the immigrants according to norms favored by the nation's old Protestant elite. This movement intensified after 1914, when the outbreak of war in Europe rendered suspect the dual loyalties perceived in immigrants from the German and Austrian empires. Kallen, a Jew born in Germany, defended the right of immigrants to resist assimilation and to maintain cohesive communities devoted to the perpetuation of ancestral religious, linguistic, and social practices. Hence the vision of America as a political canopy providing protection for a variety of descent-defined groups was the dialectical product of a distinctive historical moment: a moment at which unprecedented ethno-racial diversity collided with an Anglo-conformist movement made more aggressive by World War I.

Kallen's constitutionally vague references to the United States as a "federation" of enduring ethno-racial groups located him at the protoseparatist extreme of cultural pluralism, but his celebration of group differences appealed to a number of liberal intellectuals who shared his opposition to forced assimilation. These included John Dewey, who, without invoking either cosmopolitanism or pluralism, took friendly issue with Kallen along the lines of exactly this distinction. Dewey warned Kallen against the danger of endorsing "segregation" and of promoting a program whereby traditional cultural differences would be too rigidly "fastened upon" people.[19] Kallen's sympathizers also included Jane Addams, Louis Brandeis, and, above all, Randolph Bourne, who acknowledged Kallen as the inspiration for his legendary essay of 1916, "Trans-National America."[20]

Bourne celebrated the deprovincializing effect of immigrants on the native-born population and hailed a new, "cosmopolitan" America as superior to the more homogeneous societies left behind by the immigrants. Bourne's sense of cosmopolitanism was much thicker than the one that prevailed in Melville's time. For Bourne, cosmopolitanism implied strength and resilience rather than a lack of deep character. Cosmopolitans engaged a world the complexity of which rendered provincial tastes and skills inadequate and uninspiring. Although Bourne saw himself as an ally of Kallen's against the proponents of forced assimilation and Anglo-Saxon cultural arrogance, the drift of his argument was actually quite different from Kallen's. While Kallen stressed the autonomy and persistence of the different cultures brought to America by distinctive immigrant groups, Bourne emphasized the dynamic mixing that would change the immigrants as well as the descendants of the Pilgrims and the Founding Fathers. At some moments in "Trans-National America," to be sure, Bourne spoke in a pluralist rather than a cosmopolitan mode, endorsing the integrity of immigrant cultures and lamenting their dilution in the mass of American society. Hence the mixing of pluralism with cosmopolitanism so common in our multiculturalist debates can be found in the most significant piece of writing by multiculturalism's most illustrious precursor and prophet: Bourne himself.

In the era of World War I and the 1920s, there were few incentives to distinguish between pluralist and cosmopolitan visions of an ideal America. On the contrary, there was a common enemy to fight: the nativism that was displayed in a flourishing Ku Klux Klan and that triumphed in the Johnson-Reed Act, the congressional decision of 1924 that drastically curtailed immigration. Hence the chief, joint legacy of both Kallen's and Bourne's writings, within the small circle who read their work at all, was a simple, unelaborated insistence that American nationality should not entail the suppression of diversity nor of multiple identity.

This critique of intolerance, of prejudice, of ethnocentrism, and of one hundred percent Americanism was routinely advanced by a vocal minority of liberal and radical intellectuals during the 1930s. The most popular Broadway production during that decade, Ann Nichols's comedy *Abie's Irish Rose*, celebrated cross-ethnic love and marriage. This ideology of tolerance often carried the implicitly hierarchical assumption that some groups were more fully in possession of the nation than others. It expressed a kind of *noblesse oblige* to tolerate the rest, and was then taken up with enthusiasm by the popular media during World War II. The government recognized the propaganda value of this ideology for the purpose of mobilizing Americans of all ethno-racial identities against the Axis powers.

The classic foxhole society of wartime movies consisted of an Anglo-Protestant soldier surrounded by comrades representing Irish, Jewish, Italian, and other ethnic groups. In *Bataan* (1943), Sgt. Bill Dana (Robert Taylor) and his melting-pot comrades were all united, to be sure, by their colorfully expressed hatred of "Japs." This company of American fighting men included Desi Arnez, who played the group's Latino member.

But neither *Bataan* nor *Back to Bataan* (1945), with Anthony Quinn now playing the swarthy character, nor the other films in this popular genre, challenged the individualist and ultimately assimilationist presuppositions that Kallen's formulation of cultural pluralism had called into question. On the contrary, what celebration there was of ethno-racial groups in the World War II era was generally cast in an Americans-all idiom, aimed not at reinforcing ethno-racial affiliation but at affirming a transethnic vision of American nationality against Anglo-Protestant ethnocentrism. This was true of *One Nation,* for example, the war-inspired picture of American society the young Wallace Stegner edited for *Look* magazine.[21] *Common Ground* was the appropriately universalist title for the journal edited during the 1940s by Louis Adamic, a Slovenian immigrant now remembered as the era's most prolific advocate of an ethno-racially diverse America.

Kallen himself, in the meantime, had lost interest in these issues, married the daughter of a Methodist minister, and from the late 1920s until his death in 1974 did almost nothing to clarify cultural pluralism as a positive program. When the term *cultural pluralism* did appear during the 1930s and 1940s, it was commonly used in reference to religious rather than ethno-racial diversity. Ecumenists eager to promote cooperation between Protestants, Catholics, and Jews found the term useful.[22]

Bourne had died in 1919, but his cosmopolitanism was

espoused in the 1930s and 1940s by a substantial cohort of intellectuals engaged by two major international movements, socialism in politics and modernism in the arts.[23] Both of these movements were of course more species centered than ethnos centered, and in that respect were part of the same atmosphere for which Kinsey, Willkie, and Steichen are convenient emblems. These modernist and socialist intellectuals, many of whom were associated with the *Partisan Review,* continued Bourne's antagonism against provincialism of all sorts. The provincialism they most feared was that of traditional Anglo-Protestant nativism, but they were also critical of the provincialism of the immigrant groups, including the Jewish community into which many of these intellectuals had been born. The *Partisan Review* intellectuals did not share Adamic's warm engagement with the various ethnic cultures found within the United States, but the perspective of these proudly elitist intellectuals was more aloof than hostile. Although *Partisan Review* and *Common Ground* might be construed as vehicles for cosmopolitan and pluralist ideas, respectively, the two were not ranged against each other. *Common Ground* was much more engaged than was *Partisan Review* with American politics and with the injustices suffered by black Americans, but both stood for diversity against a continuing, if somewhat diminished, Anglo-Protestant chauvinism.

An ideology of tolerance remained a prominent feature of American intellectual life through the 1950s and 1960s, but this ideology's ties to cultural pluralism became more attenuated. Neither Kallen's name nor the term he contributed figured prominently during this postwar era. Even Will Herberg's *Protestant-Catholic-Jew*, perhaps the closest thing to a major pluralist work of the 1950s, defended an explicitly religious pluralism and invoked cultural pluralism by name only as a ghost of the 1920s. Indeed, Herberg patronized cultural pluralists as "backward-looking romantics" and "shrewd opportunists."[24]

During these twenty-five years following World War II, moreover, advocates of racial equality increasingly directed their energies against a specific target that had been of little concern to the cultural pluralists of the 1910s and 1920s: antiblack racism and the political and social inequalities resulting from it. Any movement to replace segregation with integration had little incentive to embrace the pluralist emphasis on the autonomy and durability of ethno-racial groups. The United States Supreme Court's rejection of the separate-but-equal standard in 1954 was an invitation not to difference-asserting pluralism but to engagement, if not intimacy, across the color line.

Cultural pluralism had thus become ancient history by the early 1970s, by which time a number of historic turns produced a new willingness to explore pluralist ideas. Among these turns were an extensive reconsideration of integrationist goals and strategies on the part of frustrated black leaders, the backlash against affirmative action on the part of white ethnics suddenly eager to proclaim the solidarity of their own groups, and the dramatic increase in immigration from Asian and Latin American countries facilitated by congressional action taken in 1965. The revision of immigration legislation not only increased the number of diverse ethno-racial groups substantially present in the American population but, by maintaining a steady flow of immigrants fresh from each source, provided such groups with identity reinforcement absent for most groups since Congress had suspended massive immigration in 1924. An interest in maintaining the integrity of ethno-racial communities was also stimulated, less directly, by the Vietnam War, which generated among many younger Americans a deep skepticism about the society into which peoples of all ethno-racial affiliations had been encouraged to assimilate. If the center of the society was so badly flawed, the periphery presented itself as a source of potentially countervailing cultural power.

These matrices were conducive to the initiatives of the 1970s and 1980s, which were occasionally called cultural pluralism, especially by older discussants, but which eventually came to be known as multiculturalism. The term *pluralism* had by then become associated, in academic circles at least, with a relatively uncritical perspective on the American political system as one that delivered its services reasonably well to organized interests. Had Kallen's trail been warmer and had interest-group pluralism not tainted the word "pluralism," it is possible that "cultural pluralism" rather than "multiculturalism" would have been more consistently applied to these new initiatives. They quickly took specific form in relation to the ethno-racial pentagon designed to facilitate antidiscrimination policies. A truly national debate on these cultural initiatives gave the concept of multiculturalism much more prominence than the concept of cultural pluralism had ever enjoyed.

The two movements—the multiculturalism of recent decades and the cultural pluralism of the World War I era—differed dramatically in their relation to perceived political and economic inequalities. These inequalities were generally overlooked by the cultural pluralists, but multiculturalists examined them explicitly and extensively. Indeed multiculturalism was frequently advanced as a means of empowering young people said to be psychologically victimized by a Eurocentric curriculum that displayed few achievements by members of their own ethno-racial groups. Cultural pluralism as developed by Kallen and his contemporaries was exclusively European in scope; from the perspective of multiculturalism, Europe was just one of many sources for the culture of the United States. The cultural pluralists' relative lack of attention to African Americans, in particular, renders ironic the fact that it was a black contemporary of theirs, W. E. B. Du Bois, who formulated in *The Souls of Black Folk* the notion of dual identity in terms that would become highly influential among multiculturalists.[25] As an intellectual movement, the multiculturalism of the last quarter of the twentieth century thus took on a shape and character rather different from that of the cultural pluralism of the century's early decades.

The most striking difference of all between these two episodes in the American discussion of diversity was the sheer triumph, in late-twentieth-century America, of the doctrine that the United States ought to sustain rather than diminish a great variety of distinctive cultures carried by ethno-racial groups. In the 1990s doubts about this doctrine had not disappeared, but a sea change had taken place since 1924 when Kallen, at the crest of the tide of Anglo-Protestant nativism, actually gave the doctrine the first of its two names. By the 1990s opponents of this idea were very much on the defensive in national politics, the mass media, public education, and academia. Cultural pluralism had been a minor movement in the history of the American academic and literary intelligentsia. By contrast, multiculturalism has proved to be a major preoccupation in American life as registered in the deliberations of local school boards and in the professional journals of the humanities and social sciences.

The triumph of basic multiculturalism has fostered a sensitivity to diversity so acute that the deep differences between the various groups and subgroups are now being addressed with unprecedented ethnographic detail and theoretical sophistication.[26] The communities credited with creating and sustaining the nation's many cultures have assumed their present shape in response to very different historical forces, including enslavement, conquest, and immigration under widely varying socioeconomic conditions. The more these differences have come to be recognized, the more difficult it has become to convincingly represent American society in classically pluralist fashion as an expanse of internally homogeneous and analogically structured units, each authorized by an ancestral charter and each possessed of a singular mythology of diaspora. The historical experiences of African Americans, Mexican Americans, Korean Americans, and Norwegian Americans do not fit the same abstract model.

The heightened sensitivity to diversity fostered by multiculturalism has had the ironic result of diversifying diversity to the point that the ethno-racial pentagon can no longer contain it. The most dramatic indicator of this diversification of diversity has been the demand for recognition voiced by mixed-race Americans whose affirmation of their own difference has complicated the argument over what kinds of sameness and what kinds of difference matter. "We don't want *that* kind of diversity," defenders of the ethno-racial pentagon say, in effect, to mixed-race activists, "because it undermines the sameness necessary for identity." Hence the concerns voiced by Arthur M. Schlesinger, Jr., and others on behalf of America—in, for example, Schlesinger's best-selling 1992 book, *The Disuniting of America*—can be voiced on behalf of several blocs of the pentagon. Conservative ethno-racial politicians thus play Schlesinger to the mixed-race radical disuniters.

The historian Nash is far from the only participant in the multiculturalist debates to advance explicitly the concept of cosmopolitanism in the setting of the diversification of diversity. Although the literary critic Bruce Robbins has described cosmopolitanism as an "unfashionable term that needs defending," Robbins's own vigorous and discerning defense of it[27] is but one of a number that have suddenly appeared in the quarterlies and op-ed pages, distant from the supermarket checkout counters where *Cosmopolitan* is a magazine for women with interests more careerist and provocatively sexual than the sensibility to which the nearby competitor *Family Circle* openly appeals. Political philosophers Jeremy Waldron and Mitchell Cohen have produced ringing vindications of cosmopolitanism, as have the literary theorist Tobin Siebers, the historian Linda Kerber, and the legal scholar Bruce Ackerman.[28] No doubt Helen Gurley Brown's "Cosmo girl" has an unbreakable lock on the notion of cosmopolitanism in mass culture and gives the notion some of the connotations of lightness current in Melville's time. But this complication has not prevented others from using "cosmopolitanism" to advance a vision of diversity much broader and deeper than the personal and social fulfillments exemplified by Brown's popular heroine.

Beyond the many cases in which the word *cosmopoli-*
tanism is conspicuously displayed in relation to the multiculturalist debates, one can find many expressions of frustration with identity politics or with the narrowness of these
debates that translate easily into cosmopolitan terms.[29]
"The cult of particularity and difference," complains the
geographer Yi-Fu Tuan in the midst of an appreciation for a
balancing of the local and the universal, "hinders the development of any large, liberating vision that encompasses the
stranger."[30] Some problems are actually "non-local," the literary critic David Simpson notes as if he were suddenly
awakening from a long, local slumber; perhaps the time has
come, Simpson wonders, to try again to "think big."[31] It
would be a mistake to claim that a single point of view
informs the recent writings of Marshall Berman, Angela
Davis, Andrew Delbanco, Morris Dickstein, Todd Gitlin,
Robert Hughes, and Itabari Njeri.[32] Yet these scholars, critics, and journalists, while disagreeing among themselves on
many issues and while having a variety of different priori-
ties, do seem to me to betray a cosmopolitan impatience
with some of the pluralist tendencies within multiculturalism. One way to act on this impatience is to develop a
postethnic perspective.

CHAPTER 5

Toward a Postethnic
Perspective

The diversification of diversity confronts us with some basic truths easily missed while we are simply affirming the existence and value of a multitude of cultures. The communities that are the primary sites for the formation of our identities, for the working out of our politics, and for the clarification of our moral and cognitive standards can have very different structures, shapes, and purposes. These communities come into being under a great variety of circumstances, are perpetuated for many distinctive ends, and are driven by very different distributions of power. Determining who is "us" and who is "them" can be a very different matter from case to case depending on the kind of "we" at issue. Does the salient "we" consist of Chicanos or of Texans, of geologists or of scientists, of Presbyterians or of Christians, of Americans or of human beings?

Our communities are various in their structure and function. Not all entail the same mix of voluntary and involuntary affiliation, nor do all require the same measure of internal agreement, the same sorts of demands on the individual member, or the same degree of clarity in external boundaries. No sooner do we ask, "How wide the circle of the we?" than we ought to ask, "What identifies the we?" and "How deep the structure of power within it?" and "How is the authority to set its boundaries distributed?"

A postethnic perspective recognizes that most individuals live in many circles simultaneously and that the actual living of any individual life entails a shifting division of labor between the several "we's" of which the individual is a part. How much weight at what particular moments is assigned to the fact that one is Pennsylvania Dutch or Navajo relative to the weight assigned to the fact that one is also an American, a lawyer, a woman, a Republican, a Baptist, and a resident of Minneapolis? It is this process of consciously and critically locating oneself amid these layers of "we's" that most clearly distinguishes the postethnic from the unreconstructed universalist. The latter will be tempted to try to build life-projects outside of, rather than through, particular communities. On the other hand, the willingness of the postethnic to treat ethnic identity as a question rather than as a given also helps to distinguish the postethnic from the unreconstructed ethnocentrist for whom ethnic identity is a more settled proposition, often entailing the acceptance of ostensibly primordial ties.[1]

A postethnic perspective recognizes the psychological value and political function of bounded groups of affiliation, but it resists a rigidification of the ascribed distinctions between persons that universalists and cosmopolitans have so long sought to diminish. Angela Davis exemplifies this spirit of resistance when she asks that the "ropes" attached to the "anchors" locating individuals in primary communities be long enough to enable people "to move into other communities."[2] Multiculturalism breeds an enthusiasm for specific, traditional cultures that can sometimes mask a provinciality from which individuals are eager to escape through new, out-group affiliations. Welcome as is the cultivation of difference against the conformist imperative for sameness too often felt in American society, that very imperative for sameness can all too easily be reinscribed, in yet more restrictive terms, within the cultures of smaller, particular communities. Postethnicity projects a more diverse basis for diversity than a multiplicity of ethnocentrisms can provide.

A postethnic perspective also tries to remain alert to features of any given ethnos that are common to one or more other ethnoi inclined to see each other as opposed. Kiev and Kokomo have less in common than Willkie supposed, but that need not mean we have no basis for theorizing about, and acting upon, needs and interests found to be shared by some inhabitants of these two sites. The "hero" reappearing behind "a thousand faces" may have been less monolithic than Joseph Campbell thought, but inquiry into continuities across cultures still promises to help identify features of human life that are prominently and extensively developed within populations open to historical or contemporary scrutiny. Part of the recognition of the complex character of different communities is the acceptance of the possibility that some will have closely comparable aspects and may even be able to act together on specific issues.

This sensitivity to the potentially overlapping character of various local communities is appropriately matched with a recognition of the reality and influence of communities global in scale. Jeremy Waldron has ridiculed the fantasy of some communitarians that the individual is constituted through his belonging to one homogeneous group or another:

> Think how much we owe in history and heritage—in the culture, or the cultures that have formed us—to the international communities that have existed among merchants, clerics, lawyers, agitators, scholars, scientists, writers, and diplomats. . . . We are made by our languages, our literature, our cultures, our science, our religions, our civilization. . . . We owe a debt to the world and to the global community and civilization, as well as whatever we owe to any particular region, country, nation, or tribe.[3]

❖   ❖   ❖

If these various observations in the wake of the diversification of diversity have a truistic ring, they can serve all the
better to remind us of the strength of the resources on
which one might draw while scrutinizing the enclosures
licensed by our new respect for boundaries. There are contexts in which even species-centered discourse might be
critically and cautiously renewed. One such context is
surely the physical health of the planet. Analyses of the
globe's ecological trajectories render the notion of a
specieswide interest strikingly authentic and help to neutralize the old suspicion that such universalist notions must
always be a mask for some smaller, more particular interest.
Disagreements between rich and poor nations about how to
balance development with environmental protection complicate, but do not invalidate, the insight expressed in the
environmentalist slogan, "One Earth, One Humanity, One
Destiny." That there is something almost universal about
the planet has troubled a number of commentators on the
tendency of ethnos-centered discourse to treat the world as
a set of constructions rooted in one ethnos or another.
"From the perspective of social construction," one consci-
entious and informed student of recent intellectual trends
has wondered aloud, "how do we theorize the ecological
crisis?"[4]

A postethnic perspective tries to bring to issues of affiliation a consciousness of the increasing interdependence of

the world's peoples, and of the global arena in which many of the forces that affect the lives of individuals and groups in our society, as well as in others, are generated and played out. The geographer David Harvey advocates such a consciousness in his omnivorous account of the state of the contemporary world, *The Condition of Postmodernity*. Harvey believes this consciousness is threatened by postmodernism, which, complains Harvey,

> has us accepting the reifications and partitionings, actually celebrating the activity of masking and cover-up, all the fetishisms of locality, place, or social grouping, while denying that kind of meta-theory which can grasp the political-economic processes (money flows, international divisions of labour, financial markets, and the like) that are becoming ever more universalizing in their depth, intensity, reach and power over daily life.[5]

Among the global forces that affect us are the natural objects studied by scientists. Hence communities of scientists are among the communities that a postethnic perspective most wants to protect against an excessive ethnocentrism. Professional communities in the natural sciences have proven able to successfully warrant their major claims in many locales and to acculturate persons born and raised in a multitude of tribes and clubs throughout the world. Many of us in the humanities and in the humanistically oriented social sciences are now proficient in detecting parochialism and prejudice in even the natural sciences, and highly conscious of the status of these sciences as historically specific, discursive practices. As a result, we risk losing sight of the relative success of these sciences in making their ideas work experimentally and in incorporating within their "we" a great variety of men—and more recently, women—with diverse ethno-racial and national-cultural affiliations.

All perspectives may be partial, but some are more partial than others. A postethnic orientation toward epistemic communities recognizes, rather than trivializes, the remarkable successes of the modern natural sciences. But it takes those successes as problems for theory and as challenges for politics rather than as proof that traditional and existing scientific communities have pushed the epistemic "we" as far as it can go. There may be a good bit more pushing to be done, and the resulting knowledge may serve more of the species than has been served by the knowledge we already have. A postethnic perspective seeks to test more systematically the limits of the epistemic "we" and to stretch its circle as widely as the capacities of nature and its knowers will allow.

That these capacities have their limits, and that we should not be deceived into thinking we somehow "make it all up" depending on our "regime of truth," is sometimes acknowledged even by theorists of science who have worked the hardest to explain the impact of ethno-racial and gender biases on existing scientific knowledge. Among these is Donna Haraway, whose study of the development of the discipline of primatology in its cultural context has become one of the most widely discussed of postmodernist histories of science. "Feminists have to insist on a better account of the world," Haraway has demanded. "It is not enough to show radical historical contingency and modes of construction for everything." We ought to be able to combine

> an account of radical historical contingency for all knowledge claims and knowing subjects, a critical practice for recognizing our own "semiotic technologies" for making meanings, *and* a no-nonsense commitment to faithful accounts of a "real" world, one that can be partially shared and friendly to earthwide projects of finite freedom, adequate material abundance, modest meaning in suffering and limited happiness.[6]

When someone concludes that an account is "faithful," that an idea "works" scientifically, in the context of what specific aims can one justify this conclusion? And when we observe that professional communities have managed to acculturate a demographically diverse population of men and women, just what elements in that human diversity are silenced in the interests of perpetuating the success of existing research programs? And how might these elements be given greater voice in order to generate and vindicate new and alternative research programs? These questions are being formulated and pursued by Nancy Cartwright, Peter Galison, Ian Hacking, Margaret Jacob, Evelyn Fox Keller, Theodore Porter, Robert Proctor, Steven Shapin, Londa Shiebinger, and a host of other historians and philosophers of science who know inquiry to be situated but who resist facile constructions of the relevant situations in terms of uncritically defined and self-enclosed social-cognitive units. The work of these scholars sustains the hope that the knowledge sought by science can still—in this age of historicism—be construed as ideally public, subject to verification by anyone comparably equipped, trained, and positioned.[7]

An inclination toward such stretching of the "we" is also what a postethnic perspective brings to moral communities. Controversies over the welfare of non-Western women have recently dramatized the difficulties in determining the extent of a circle within which we feel obligations and feel a right to judge others for failing to meet such obligations. Alice Walker's *Possessing the Secret of Joy*, which takes a highly judgmental view of the treatment of women in a culture distant from her own, is but the most widely noted example of this controversy.[8]

If the Masai women of east Africa are but breeding stock, and, when barren of sons, are treated by their warrior masters as inferior to cattle, who are we to criticize? It's part of Masai culture, after all. And we probably should not even talk about it, as such talk might flatter Western prejudice and might lead us to forget how much violence and injustice are suffered by women in the United States and western Europe. If one is looking for people with contrasting values, or looking for evils licensed by cultural difference, one does not have to go to Africa.

This easy way out begs the larger question: is Africa to be excluded and avoided? Am I my sister's keeper, and if I am, who is my sister? A clitoridectomy performed in a Muslim neighborhood in Paris is no doubt more easily condemned than if the operation is performed in Sudan. But where does a respect for the taboos, practices, and inhibitions of other cultures come into play?

Many who take an interest in the victims of "genital mutilation" are also sensitive to the particularity of the cultures with which women as well as men must deal, and they are reluctant to dismiss as false consciousness the insistence by some Saudi and Sudanese women that Western feminists have no authority to instruct them on their rights, needs, and duties.[9] The project of trying to mobilize sentiment against clitoridectomy within the societies in which it is practiced partakes of an old missionary ethos, according to which "we" try to persuade "them" that they would be better off doing some things more the way we do because they and we are ultimately part of the same larger, human community.

Trying to reason with members of other tribes, trying to get them to recognize common interests, and even trying to convince them that they might be better off by adopting our own ways is an ideal easily dismissed. Yet this old ideal is now being advanced with force and conviction by Jurgen Habermas, Jeffrey Stout, and others, whose project of building a community through intersubjective reason would seem aimed exactly at the goal that even Rorty has now acknowledged as his own: the expansion of "our" democratic-egalitarian ethnos through immanent critique and the expansion of a "human rights culture" as far as social circumstances will permit it to spread.[10]

The political theorist Selya Benhabib speaks in what I take to be a postethnic idiom when she defends a moral criticism that is "situated" yet unafraid to address the interests of a "global community." Just because certain feminist ideas appear to "only articulate the sensitivities of white, middle-class, affluent, first world, heterosexual women," insists Benhabib, we should not ignore the potential of these ideas as resources for advancing the cause of the liberation of women in a yet-to-be determined range of specific contexts. Sometimes we must not "shy away" from knocking down the "parish walls."[11]

Nor must we shy away from pushing against the walls dividing up the ethno-racial pentagon, and perhaps knocking some holes in them. If a postethnic perspective brings to moral and epistemic communities a disposition to stretch the "we," so, too, does this perspective bring to the question of affiliation within the United States a sense that the prevailing enclosures are too narrow, too uncritically accepted, too difficult to open and realign, and are made to serve too many different purposes simultaneously.

The essence of this postethnic perspective on affiliation within American society has already been set forth at several points in this book. Postethnicity prefers voluntary to prescribed affiliations, appreciates multiple identities, pushes for communities of wide scope, recognizes the constructed character of ethno-racial groups, and accepts the formation of new groups as a part of the normal life of a democratic society. It may clarify the character and significance of these preferences to point out that none of them would have appealed to Horace Kallen. The great pluralist thought he had made an unanswerable argument for the primacy of primordial ethno-racial identities when he observed that one thing no one can change is his or her grandfather. A postethnic perspective challenges the right of one's grandfather or grandmother to determine primary identity. Individuals should be allowed to affiliate or disaffiliate with their own communities of descent to an extent that they choose, while affiliating with whatever nondescent communities are available and appealing to them.

The postethnic preference for choice over prescription does not carry with it any lack of appreciation for commitments that truly bind. People often need to make commitments that others can count on. Postethnicity does not project a society in which people change all their commitments as easily as they might change styles in clothing or music. The adopting of a child from a different "race" than oneself is a very postethnic act by virtue of its refusal to allow the social bond to be determined by the genetic bond, but this act carries a lifetime commitment. Postethnicity reacts not against commitment but against prescribed affiliations on the basis of descent. When Joseph Raz defends a "right of exit" from the group,[12] he argues against the still popular Kallenesque presumption that grandparents are destiny.

A postethnic perspective recognizes that choices are made in specific, limiting circumstances, some of which are ancestral. Grandparents do help to create a frame for life, along with parents and one's entire familial background, cultural as well as genetic. One does not easily choose to be a Japanese American in the absence of an element of Japanese ancestry to begin with. Moreover, it would be silly to suggest that one can make a viable life out of any materials gathered purely at random, or to deny that one's gatherings are directed by whatever sense of identity a person possesses while doing the gathering. The communitarian theorist Michael Sandel is right to declare that a life with any depth and "character" entails the knowledge that "I move in a history I neither summon nor command, which carries consequences none the less for my choices and conduct."[13]

But this insight does not carry us very far. The issue is

how much choice there is in relation to given desires. Sandel's dictum does not provide an answer to this question, but only a sensible caution against the fantasy that we can make our lives out of whole cloth. The same warning was once issued even more eloquently by a thinker more sympathetic than Sandel to Promethean aspirations: human beings "make their own history," wrote Karl Marx, "but they do not make it just as they please, they do not make it under circumstances chosen by themselves, but under circumstances directly encountered, given, and transmitted from the past."[14]

The principle that ethno-racial affiliations should be subject to revocable consent is a modest choice-maximizing principle based on the presumption that people—especially Americans who can invoke the constitutional tradition of the United States—ought to be more free than they now are from social distinctions visited upon them by others. Postethnicity aims not at the diminution of communities of descent; it aims, rather, at the renewal and critical revision of those communities of descent whose progeny choose to devote their energies to these communities even after experiencing opportunities for affiliating with other kinds of people. Not every descent-community will retain its members; some of these communities can be expected, over time, to decrease their role in the lives of individuals and of the larger society. New affiliations gradually replace old and eventually come to be called ethnic.

A postethnic perspective denies neither history nor biology—nor the need for affiliations—but it does deny that history and biology provide a set of clear orders for the affiliations we are to make. This perspective does challenge, very directly, a common prejudice to the effect that affiliations based on choice are somehow artificial and lacking in depth, while those based on the ordinance of blood and history are more substantive and authentic.[15] Boundaries between groups deserve more, rather than less, respect according to the degree to which these boundaries reflect the will of the people bound by them. There is certainly too much superficiality in the world, but superficiality does not follow from volition any more than authenticity follows from submission to tradition and authority. We should not "denigrate the capacity of people to change the definitions of the boundaries around them," insists the sociologist Alan Wolfe; "for every boundary that is ascribed, others can be achieved."[16]

A postethnic perspective does not suppose that boundaries of the same order will work for everyone, nor that communities of the same scope and scale are right for all. Personal psychology and taste as well as educational, economic, and political conditions obviously affect this issue in any given case. Few people will ever choose to model themselves on a supercosmopolitan like the London-based, Bombay-born Salman Rushdie, who describes his *Satanic Verses* as a vindication of virtues he has tried to exemplify in his own life: "hybridity, impurity, intermingling . . . and mongrelization." Yet it is exactly these lines from Rushdie's cosmopolitan manifesto, *In Good Faith,* that come to the mind of ethnologist Karen Leonard when she sums up the meaning of the lives of the rural Californians who have changed inherited boundaries to create the Punjabi-Mexican community. This community has been formed out of immigrant communities of south Asians and Mexicans. The men and women who made the Punjabi-Mexican community are themselves "creative producers of new identities," insists Leonard, "agents in the shaping of our contemporary world." If Rushdie is a hero to metropolitan intellectuals who count both New York and Paris as home, Rushdie is also a prophet for Leonard's farmers and restauranteurs, who in Yuba City and El Centro live out Rushdie's belief that "melange, hotch-potch, a bit of this and that is *how newness enters the world.*"[17]

One specific variety of boundary achieving worth mentioning here is the kind found in the making of religion and in the decisions individuals make about religious affiliation. Our multiculturalist debates, dominated by the presumption that culture is largely an ethno-racial phenomenon, have rarely addressed religion.[18] Religious affiliations, like ethno-racial ones, have histories; religions are usually chosen in contexts that presume that an individual will follow in the religious orientation of his or her parents. But the right of exit is more widely accepted in relation to religious than to ethno-racial communities. So, too, is it generally accepted that the degree of involvement in a religious community can vary enormously. Moreover, the depth of this involvement is often greater among converts than among birthright members of a particular religious community.

A multiculturalism less conspicuously aloof from religious cultures would necessarily engage the right of exit, and also the dynamics of entry. Religious groups in America have certainly had their exclusions—often ethno-racial—but even the least evangelical of Protestant groups, such as the Episcopalians and Unitarians, have generally prided themselves on welcoming newcomers to their particular community of faith. Protestant denominationalism in America continues to be a historic case of largely voluntary affiliation taking place within a distinctive social and intellectual framework that promotes some choices and discourages others. The Roman Catholic Church, moreover, has long been one of the most demographically comprehensive voluntary associations in the United States. The Islamic faith is one of the most rapidly growing fellowships in this society. Even most varieties of Judaism, a more descent-defined religion, are open to converts.

To think of religious affiliations and ethno-racial affiliations as comparable requires the placing in brackets of a host of traits that distinguish the two. But this heuristic exercise may produce some interesting results. One result might be the conclusion that religious groups merit some of the status and protection now afforded to ethno-racial groups. Some evangelical Christians have already proposed this and have offered themselves as the newest minority in need of protection to guarantee their cultural equality and to facilitate their survival in the face of a secular intellectual establishment. The separation between church and state should not be construed as a barrier, it is said, to federal support for educational institutions that require adherence to certain religious doctrines.[19]

In this view, the blurring of the line between religious and ethno-racial affiliations serves to make over religious groups in the contemporary image of ethno-racial minorities. The increasingly cultural valence of the ethno-racial pentagon provides this potential opportunity for a group to claim through its cultural role in a diverse society some of the protections that attend on holding minority space within a pentagon designed to facilitate the correction of abuses that follow from ascribed categories. This is to see religion in terms of an ethnic model of affiliations within the United States, with the understanding that ethnic affiliation holds a promise of entitlement that religious affiliation does not.

An element of exactly this way of thinking is already embodied in the rights Amish communities have been guaranteed by courts in the interests of enabling the Amish to perpetuate themselves as a distinctive social community. Amish children are not obliged to attend school beyond the

education provided within the Amish communities themselves, in order that they not be exposed to the wider world.
But these rights to remain apart, as clarified in *Wisconsin v.
Yoder,* apply to a group willing to rigidly separate itself from
the larger society.[20] What if a group wanting to use public
schools asks for comparable protection of their way of life
in that more public setting, demanding that schools diminish attention to ideas that threaten this group? So far, suits
asking this have been unsuccessful.[21] But a softer version of
the same logic would simply give greater curricular attention to the ideas and values of religious communities represented in a given district or region, just as schools are often
encouraged to develop course materials reflecting the
ethno-racial composition of a local community. The widespread enthusiasm for creationism and for school prayer
indicates how strong is the constituency ready to take
advantage of whatever openings might follow from the
application to religious affiliations of the ethnic-minority
paradigm.[22]

But one can instead reason in the opposite direction
and apply to ethno-racial affiliations a religious paradigm.
The implications of this approach are quite different, especially in view of the principle of the separation of church
and state. Ethno-racial affiliations have come to play a role
similar to that played by religious affiliations at the time of
the founding of the republic and throughout most of American history. It follows, then, that some of the guarded-but-

respectful attitude toward religious cultures expressed in the Constitution—and in the history of church-state decisions by courts—might now be judiciously directed toward ethno-racial groups in their capacity as vehicles for culture.

In this second view, ethno-racial cultures ought to look after themselves much the way religious cultures have been expected to do. Both are sustained by voluntary affiliations. The products of both are to be welcomed as contributions to the richness of the nation's cultural life and thus as part of the environment for its politics. But both partake more of the private than the public sphere, and neither is to be the beneficiary of outright public subsidies. In the meantime, programs for affirmative action can continue to occupy the political space that was theirs alone before culture began to take over the ethno-racial pentagon.

Movement in this second direction—the religious model for ethno-racial cultures rather than the ethnic model for religious cultures—might reduce some of the pressure on public schools and on higher education to satisfy the need for cultural self-validation on the part of ethno-racial groups. It might also turn educational policy toward explorations and displays of cultural diversity that are less politically pretentious. To the extent that educators can be relieved of some of their implicit responsibility for ensuring that the nation's several communities of descent prosper, educators may be less tempted to divide up the entirety of culture into politically functional ethno-racial segments.

No doubt the bulk of the worthy educational innovations inspired by multiculturalism could be justified within a moderately scaled-down understanding of what cultural services schools are expected to provide. The textbooks for the study of American history written by Gary Nash and his collaborators, for example, could certainly be so justified.[23] One can write narratives calculated to include without turning the past into a retrospective mirror of the ethno-racial present. A variety of revisions of canons and curricula now provide our schools with a more accurate and comprehensive vision of American life. The inadequate attention to the cultural contributions of ethno-racial minorities was a failing much in need of correction, and our scholars and educators have applied themselves to this task with great success in the 1970s, 1980s, and 1990s. But de-escalating the political expectations of culture makes it easier to proceed without implicitly or explicitly regarding each segment of the curriculum as the meeting of an obligation to one or another of the blocs of the pentagon.[24] An interesting example of this problem is the nation's standard democratic-egalitarian ideals. Are they not European?

Whatever the ultimate origins and sustaining conditions of the ideals of democracy and equality as now understood in the United States, these ideals have become available in twentieth-century America through routes that are overwhelmingly Anglo-American and western European. It should not follow that Euro-Americans of today have a greater claim on these ideals than does anyone else. But if young people are encouraged to line up their culture with their genes, those within the non-European ethno-racial blocs have good reason to reserve their enthusiasm for democratic-egalitarian values until such time as evidence is produced that their own ancestral group experienced libertarian moments no less historically strategic than the actions of the Parliament of James I or the Putney Debates of the New Model Army. The historical significance of these episodes in seventeenth-century England can be contested, but Latino and Japanese American youth will presumably make up their minds about democratic-egalitarian ideals without waiting to see if scholars can find ways to downgrade the relative importance of England—and Europe generally—in the historical development and transferal to modern America of these ideals.[25] That the temptation to do just that—to reallocate the valued past to the ancestry of groups in need of empowerment—is genuine is indicated by the effort of some educators in New York State to assign to the United States Constitution an ancestry that prominently included the Iroquois confederation.[26]

This temptation, which a postethnic perspective resists, might well be called the will to descend. This is the claiming, on behalf of a particular community of descent, of contributions to civilization the value of which is already recognized in a social arena well beyond the specific community of descent seeking empowerment through genealogy.

The capacity of certain ancestors to function as cultural capital in a contemporary struggle is what renders the claiming of these ancestors a potentially empowering step. An example widely discussed in recent years is the assertion that the ancient Egyptians were black. Although this assertion is often associated with Martin Bernal's provocatively titled *Black Athena*—suggesting the possibility that the Greek culture influenced by Egypt was itself significantly black—Bernal's principal contribution is actually to show us how white scholars of more than a century ago reassigned classical Greece from a partly African and Asian ancestry long acknowledged to a new, predominantly European ancestry.[27]

Bernal's achievement reminds us that much of the culture of the West traditionally carried by American schools was already cast in ethno-racial terms and was much in need of the demystifying scrutiny to which it has been subjected in recent years. The will to descend had already been indulged, in a multitude of fields, to the benefit of Europeans and of white Americans. Correcting this need not mean cynically turning the tables and indulging this will on behalf of some other contemporary group. At issue is how much of our appreciation for a doctrine or a work of art or an institution should be based on its perceived ethno-racial ancestry. From a postethnic perspective, the answer is, not much. Certainly we want to know as much as we can about the society and culture of ancient Egypt and Greece, and we do not want racist interpretations to go uncorrected. But honest efforts to find the truth should not be understood to place at risk the relative self-esteem of black and white children in contemporary America. Egypt, surely, belongs to us all, and so, too, does democracy.

Defenders of the culture of the West need to state clearly that this culture is to be affirmed because it is valuable, not because it is Western. Whether Italy or India has been the historic site of a given idea's most energetic development need not create a compelling incentive or disincentive for any person of any descent to accept it. The evaluations we perform are of course the result of our historical circumstances, but the more self-aware we become about our historicity and the more concerned we are to check our own ethnocentrism, the more possible it should be to justify our preferences broadly. It is not a matter of liking what we know, but of knowing what we like.

The upshot of this extended example of how educational policy might be debated in a postethnic perspective is not that culture is to be divorced from politics, but that the significance of ethno-racial distinctions is not always the same in culture as it is in politics. Ethno-racial distinctions remain involuntary as they serve to identify people who need protection from discrimination. But an individual who has every right to such protection on the basis of his or her involuntary classification as a member of a historically disadvantaged ethno-racial group may have no interest whatsoever in the culture popularly associated with that group.

Or, he or she may be massively committed to that culture; but in neither case is the individual's culture relevant to the entitlement. The individual is a voluntary affiliate of the group for the purposes of culture, but for that reason is no less at risk as a perceived black, brown, red, or yellow, which are the culture-free categories that make the ethno-racial pentagon work quite well for the purpose of identifying people at risk of being discriminated against.

A truly postethnic America would be one in which the ethno-racial component in identity would loom less large than it now does in politics as well as culture, and in which affiliation by shared descent would be more voluntary than prescribed in every context. Although many middle-class Americans of European descent can now be said to be postethnic in this sense, the United States as a whole is a long way from achieving this ideal. This ideal for the American civic community is, indeed, just that—an ideal, embodying the hope that the United States can be more than a site for a variety of diasporas and of projects in colonization and conquest.

CHAPTER 6

The Ethnos, the Nation,
the World

Among the historic acts for which President Woodrow Wilson is remembered is bringing the Jim Crow system to the nation's capital. White Washingtonians did not lack means to discriminate against their black fellow citizens before Wilson came to town in 1913, but the first southerner to occupy the White House since the Civil War did come with something new: the South's system of separate-and-unequal public accommodations and services that survived until it was dismantled by protest movements and court decisions in the 1950s and 1960s. Although Wilson's institutionalization of racial segregation is sometimes seen as an anomaly in a progressive president's vision for America and the world, there is a certain logical consistency between this act and another historic act for which Wilson is also remembered: championing the cause of national self-determination on the part of the various ethnic groups of Europe after World War I.

Wilson's advocacy of the nationalism of Czechs, Poles, and other minorities within the old European empires was of course intended to liberate the downtrodden, while his advocacy of the Jim Crow system cannot be so construed. But Wilson's acts at the Versailles conference of 1919, which redrew the map of Europe, bespoke an ethnic rather than a civic nationalism, just as his commitment to racial separation in the United States compromised the nonethnic ideology of the American nation. The nations to which Wilson ascribed a right to self-determination were ethnic entities, even if some of the new states Wilson helped to create—especially Czechoslovakia and Yugoslavia—were more multiethnic than his theory warranted. Indeed, the dissolution of Czechoslovakia and Yugoslavia in our own time are events more truly Wilsonian in spirit than were these Versailles-created states to begin with.

The case of Woodrow Wilson dramatizes and renders historically concrete a distinction between ethnic and civic nations[1] essential to the development of a postethnic perspective on American nationhood and the American nation-state. Insofar as there is an ideal nation from a postethnic point of view, it is a democratic state defined by a civic principle of nationality in the hands of an ethno-racially diverse population and possessed of a national ethnos of its own. This last element—a national culture—is too often belittled by today's multiculturalists, but without it the promise of postethnic nationality can be too easily swept aside by the forces of transnational capitalism and ethno-racial particularism. In this chapter, I want to explain the appeal of postethnic nationality in a world of simultaneously globalizing and particularizing forces, and to address the United States as a powerful nation-state with the potential to exemplify postethnic nationality.

The nationalism we hear the most about today in the Balkans, in south Asia, and in the parts of Europe that were once within the Soviet Union holds ethnicity to be the proper foundation of the nation. Nationality, in this view, is based on descent. The true nation is a solidarity grounded in what its adherents understand to be primordial ties, not any instrumental or accidental connections. This type of nationalism was developed the most conspicuously in the nineteenth century by Germans, the bulk of whom were brought within a new nation-state under Prussian leadership in 1871. Today, the example of ethnic nationalism most appreciated in the United States is Israel, which is, along with Germany, one of only two states to grant a right of return to anyone classified as a "blood-carrying" member of the nation that formed the state.

Ethnic nationalism claims "that an individual's deepest attachments are inherited, not chosen," states the self-styled cosmopolitan Michael Ignatieff in his television series and book, *Blood and Belonging*, as he laments the persistence of primordially defined conflicts in Northern Ireland, Kurdistan, Quebec, and several sites in eastern Europe and the Balkans. The more precarious principle of civic nationality, according to Ignatieff, asserts

> that the nation should be composed of all those—regardless of race, color, creed, gender, language, or ethnicity—who subscribe to the nation's political creed. This nationalism is called civic because it envisages the nation as a community of equal, rights-bearing citizens, united in patriotic attachment to a shared set of political practices and values.[2]

Civic nationalism is the variety of nationalism developed the most conspicuously by the United States and France following the revolutions of 1776 and 1789, and also by the countries of Latin America who declared their independence early in the nineteenth century. The revolutionaries who created the United States and the Latin American republics "shared a common language and a common descent with those against whom they fought," Benedict Anderson has emphasized in *Imagined Communities,* the most provocative and influential book on nationalism written in our time.[3] Nationality, in this second view, is based on the principle of consent and is ostensibly open to persons of a variety of ethno-racial affiliations. A civic nation is built and sustained by people who honor a common future more than a common past. Wilson's emphasis on language and descent rendered his nationalism deeply "unamerican."

Civic nations often limit on the basis of ethno-racial prejudice the people who can consent to join them—the history of American immigration and naturalization laws and practices are a striking example—but when they do so they have to work against their own principles. Civic nations are often accused of being artificial by proponents of ethnic nationalism, for whom the civic nation lacks a proper, primordial foundation.

The challenge faced by civic nationalism in truly diverse societies is indicated by the precariousness of India's nation-state amid internal pressures from majority Hindus and a variety of ethnic and religious minorities. The universalism of the French, too, has been tested by "foreigners," especially North Africans. And the protracted failure of the United States to guarantee equal rights to many of its own citizens shows, again, the strength of the forces against which civic nationalism must struggle when it is not simply pasted over a de facto ethnic nationalism. Although a nationality that is technically civic in character now applies in Norway, Italy, Japan, and a number of other ethnically homogeneous countries, these examples are less significant because the civic principle has been able to trade on the work of social consolidation performed by ethnic solidarity over many centuries. A cynic might suggest that these societies work because their ethnic cleansing was carried out so far back in history that we no longer care or notice.

The vehemence of ethnic cleansing in Europe since 1989 has generated in some European intellectuals a neo-universalist reaction stronger even than Ignatieff's that extends to the vindication, in what might be called an American style, of hybridization. "I'm a passionate supporter of all that can ensure that tomorrow people on this continent will be hybrids," says the French philosopher Bernard-Henri Levy, for whom Europe, rather than France or humanity serves as the salient "we." Levy describes his ideal Europe as a "machine to break, complicate, reduce, and put into perspective all identities and national groups," but laments that such a Europe is generally rejected in favor of more narrowly particularist identities. "The great modern and murderous delirium in Europe is the folly of ethnic identity."[4] Some would say the same of the United States.

The United States has never been without a battle of a kind between the illegitimate ethnic nation and the official civic nation. This is the conflict, invoked in the first chapter of this book, between the nation's strictly nonethnic ideology and its extensively ethnic history. The damage the ethnic protonation of Anglo-Protestants—and later of white Americans generally—inflicted on ethnoracial groups imperfectly protected by the civic nation endows the multiculturalism of our time with its political intensity. An ironic consequence of this well-documented history is that American criticisms of the civic nation are now voiced not only by those purporting to speak on behalf of "the people who built this country" but also by persons carrying the mantle of ethno-racial minorities. If echoes of the older nativism can still be heard in some of the calls for a "more Christian America" emanating from the religious right, the tables have partly turned. The civic nation, so long accused of being too commodious, too accepting of outsiders, is now credibly accused of being too insensitive to the group needs of people who bring non-European ethnicities into the republic. The claims of diaspora and of conquered peoples are raised against pressures for assimilation.

Yet it would be a mistake to conflate America's version of the battle between the ethnic and the civic nation with the versions of this battle now being fought in Kurdistan, Bosnia, and most of the other parts of the world that generate today's headlines about nationalism. Many of those disputes feature one or more de facto ethnic nations struggling against one another, and most of them entail either the creation of new states or the drastic redrawing of state boundaries. This is simply not the situation in the United States. Even the overwhelming majority of those African American and Latino intellectuals whose programs for cultural enclaving and group entitlements lead their most hostile critics to call them separatists do not advance movements for separate sovereignty remotely comparable to that found in the Canadian province of Quebec or the Tamil region of Sri

Lanka. Incanting Bosnia or Belfast to silence people who are trying to explore the promise of ethno-racial solidarities within the United States is a too easy way out of a conversation that needs to be continued, patiently and deliberately.

Exactly what place such ethno-racial solidarities should have in any particular civic nation needs to be worked out within the circumstances of that nation. No one begins with a clean slate. No one can simply draw up any system of affiliations at all. But a civic nation can play a role in the dynamics of affiliation that an ethnic nation cannot. The civic nation is located midway, so to speak, between the ethnos and the species. It can mediate between them, and all the more significantly when the society is diverse: a civic nation mediates between the species and those ethno-racial varieties of humankind represented within its borders.

Mediation can be of many sorts. This description of civic nations as mediators fits well the old Austro-Hungarian empire, with its many semiautonomous peoples being governed by the old Hapsburg monarchy. So, too, does the description fit some of the dictatorial states of Africa that have inherited borders set by the European colonial powers. One can mediate by telling everyone what to do, by virtually ceding authority to regional or ethno-racial sovereignties, or even by establishing hierarchies of groups and systems of apartheid. The case of the Soviet Union should be of particular interest to multiculturalists.

The Soviet Union developed a civic nationalism that,

paradoxically, promoted the ethnic protonationalisms that eventually challenged and helped to destroy the Soviet Union itself. This self-contradictory episode in the history of civic nationalism remains poorly understood in the United States today. Soviet leaders from Lenin on, ambivalent toward the need for cultural particularity on behalf of the Soviet Union itself, "mediated" between the species and the ethnos by actually *subsidizing* Latvian, Georgian, Ukrainian, and other particularisms. As a result, when the extravagantly universalist Soviet polity itself—the instrument, ostensibly, for all humankind's eventual liberation—weakened at the end of the 1980s, the only cultural adhesives strong enough to mobilize collective action were ethnic.[5] The nationalisms that have emerged in the ruins of the bolshevik project amount not to the natural reappearance of pre-Soviet, primordial groups; rather, they are the ironic culmination of the Soviet cultural policy of promoting ethnic particularism.

When the role of mediation is performed by a democratic polity with universalist and egalitarian aspirations less extravagant than those of the Soviet state, however, it can be a significant step in the struggle for achieving sound affiliations. Of the various "we's" available, a civic nation with democratic aspirations and a sense of its own historical particularity can be a rather attractive candidate, given the alternatives. The philosopher Thomas Nagel has recently argued that the inherently dangerous but indispensable instinct for solidarity is better acted upon in relation to a democratic nation-state than in relation to "racial, linguistic, or religious identification" on the one hand, or "the world" on the other. The political economist Robert B. Reich's *The World of Nations: Preparing for 21st-Century Capitalism* provides a careful justification for a nation-centered answer to the question—generated by his analysis of the world capitalist economy—that forms the title of its final chapter: "Who is 'Us'?"[6] The promise at this time in history of locating primary affiliation in citizenship within a democratic nation-state is an implication of much recent work by philosophers, historians, and political economists.

The United States is not the only democratic, civic nation to mediate modestly between the species and its ethno-racial varieties. Canada is another, and examples from other continents might include Argentina, Brazil, and Zimbabwe. But the United States has exemplified both democracy and the principle of civic nationality for a longer period of time than have any of the comparably multiethnic societies. It has done so with a population more ethno-racially diverse than that of most of the comparably civic nations of the globe. And, it has maintained a greater measure of cultural particularity of its own—an American culture the depth and character of which are frequently contested, to be sure—than have most of the other, comparable entities. The national community of the United States—the "we"

that corresponds to American citizenship—*mediates more directly than most other national communities do* between the species and the ethno-racial varieties of humankind.

This is not to say "We are the world."[7] This popular trope may help us recognize the diversity within American society, but it also threatens to deceive us into supposing that the varieties of humankind are no more various than those prominently represented within the borders of the United States. It also tempts us to underestimate the cultural particularity of the United States, ignoring the continuities that cut across ethno-racial and other lines and enable people living in most of the rest of the world to identify many of us as Americans when we appear in their midst. Further, the sense that the United States is isomorphic with the world portends an imperialist propensity to take it over. The points I am making about the United States are more modest.

The United States is unusual in the extent and passion with which its ideological spokespersons accept and defend the nation's negotiated, contingent character within a broad canopy of universalist abstractions derived from the Enlightenment. "America is still a radically unfinished society," Michael Walzer has recently reminded us in tones reminiscent of Randolph Bourne's characterization of a dynamic, "transnational" America welcoming and transforming many varieties of humankind.[8] But Bourne spoke against the torrent of nativist Anglo-Saxonism that eventually curtailed immigration in the 1920s, while Walzer speaks

at the nation's touted multiculturalist moment, in an atmosphere of increasingly widespread acceptance of cultural diversity as a national virtue. The constructed, profoundly nonprimordial character of national solidarity in the United States is openly avowed and treated as a virtue rather than an embarrassing compromise.[9]

The United States is unusual, moreover, in that it is actually making some progress toward rendering its open and flexible self-image less fraudulent than it once was. A new demographic diversity—marked the most dramatically by the numbers and varieties of Asian and Latin American immigrants and their offspring now part of American society—has diminished yet further the privileged connection between American nationality and Anglo-Protestant ancestry challenged earlier by Catholics, Jews, other European ethnics, and the African American descendants of slaves. A Chinese ethnic can of course be a citizen of France or of Great Britain, or even of Israel, Austria, or Japan, but in all of these cases he or she will encounter a national community with a manifestly more ethnocentric social history and public culture than he or she will encounter in the contemporary United States. Moreover, when this Chinese ethnic, or a white southerner, or any other American rooted in any one particular enclave within the United States manages to identify with the American people as a whole, that American takes a tiny but ideologically significant step toward fraternal solidarity with the species.

To recognize this feature of American nationality need not be to minimize the reality of ethno-racial prejudice, discrimination, and violence within American society. Nor need it serve to reawaken the dangerous myth of the chosen people, bearing, in Melville's apotheosis, "the ark of the liberties of the world."[10] One can easily enumerate the failures of the American effort to "share" American liberties with the world and to guarantee these liberties to those of its own citizens lacking the privilege of Anglo-Protestant ancestry. Indeed, so conscious are many of us today of American arrogance—and so appalled at the uncritical enthusiasm for American military power displayed by much of the public during the Persian Gulf War of 1991—that we tend to avoid earnest discussions of American nationality out of fear that the topic itself can yield only chauvinism. But the ideological resources of the United States are simply too useful to democratic egalitarians to be conceded to the far Right while the rest of us devote our public energies to more narrowly particularist or more broadly universalist projects.

The value of a democratic nation-state that is commodious enough to sustain diversity yet cohesive enough to guarantee rights and provide for welfare is too easily lost from view as we try to absorb and assess the global scale on which much of life is now lived. The relative significance of the nation-state as an institution, we are told with increasing assurance and frequency, is declining proportionately with the rise in influence of transnational or postnational organizations and loyalties. But "a cosmopolitan, postnationalist spirit" still depends, as Ignatieff insists, "on the capacity of nation-states to provide security and civility for their citizens."[11]

This insight is lacking in much recent talk about the emerging postnational order, which breathes an air of political unreality. One of postnationality's most thoughtful and learned enthusiasts, the anthropologist Arjun Appadurai, describes the Olympic movement as "only the most spectacular among a series of sites and formations on which the uncertain future of the nation-state will turn."[12] But the Olympic games turn out repeatedly to serve as arenas for an exuberant nationalism in which individual athletes are virtually carried about the stadium and the world's electronic media by the flags and anthems of their sponsoring states. The Olympic spirit had an opportunity to work its wonders in Sarajevo, where its wholesome legacy is now hard to see. The Olympic movement proved unable even to prevent Tonya Harding from skating at Lillehammer after she admitted to a very non-Olympic degree of involvement in the attack on her rival, Nancy Kerrigan. The American representatives of the Olympic movement were thwarted by the threat of a civil suit; what stood in the way of the Olympic movement's enforcement of its own ideals was the American nation-state's rules for protecting the rights of its citizens.

The amount of postnational significance carried by other transnational formations Appadurai mentions is also open to question. Amnesty International, Habitat for Humanity, Oxfam, and "networks of Christian philanthropy, such as World Vision"[13] are no doubt virtuous, valuable organizations, but we should not kid ourselves about the power they wield. Appadurai is also cheered by cases of ethno-racial diasporas that do not express themselves in the form of demands for territorial states—he mentions Armenians in Turkey and Kashmiri Hindus in the Indian capital of Delhi—but these are weak indicators of the promise of a postnational order when we have before us examples of so many state-seeking and state-redesigning movements. On whom can diasporic minorities truly count for the enforcement of their rights other than the state in which they reside? And from what authority do such rights derive? The force of world opinion and of international organizations such as the United Nations does matter, but not much.

Nation-states still do matter, enormously. They are at present "the only effective political structures," insists the British sociologist Nicholas Garnham, to deal with the cultural as well as the economic dimension of globalization. Nation-states can counteract, to some extent, "the growing domination of global networks of cultural production and distribution" so that "citizens of a polity" can debate among themselves what actions they wish to take.[14] Yet the nation-state, so long a dominating presence in the world, does face pressures that are often counted as a crisis.

These pressures are invoked by two of our era's buzz-words, *globalization* and *particularization*. The capitalist economy has always been international, yet until recently most theorists of its expansion anticipated that the social and cultural peculiarities of distinctive localities would steadily diminish as a result of incorporation within a single, modern world-system. As the range and pace of economic integration has sharply increased, however, especially since the early 1970s, a host of particularist movements have resisted cultural homogenization. The strident assertion of particularity on the part of various religious, ethnic, and regional communities is stimulated in part by resistance to the Western cultural values that often come with more complete integration into the world-capitalist economy. But this particularization is sometimes actually facilitated by the strategies of globalization. In the "culture industries," observes Kevin Robins, "the drive to achieve ever greater economies of scale" dictates the targeting of "the shared habits and tastes of particular market segments at the global level" rather than at the level of geographic proximity.[15] Both local and diasporic taste-communities are thus reinforced by the sophisticated marketing strategies of multinational corporations eager to exploit a particular culture-market wherever it may be geographically located.

In this context of simultaneous globalist and particularist pressures, the link between the nation and the state may loosen.[16] Nation-states exist when the apparatus of a state is associated with a people who think of themselves as a nation, but history is filled with nations lacking states and with states lacking a population united by the strong sense of peoplehood that makes a nation. Since a state functions better if the population supports it, leaders of states are naturally eager to convince their citizens that they constitute a nation whose will is expressed by the state. Just how convincing or fraudulent are a given state's claims to speak for a nation is the perennial issue in the history of modern nationalism. This issue is acutely felt by civic nation-states being told that they embrace many nations that should, perhaps, have their own states. Whatever tensions exist within any given nation-state between its nation and its state are intensified by the dynamics of globalization and particularization. States will continue to exist, of course. What they will respond to, however, may not be a nation. It may be, instead, a multitude of constituencies united less by a sense of common destiny than by a will to use the state as an instrument of their particular agendas.

Isn't that what nation-states have always been? Some would interpret the history of the United States itself as essentially a story of successful and unsuccessful struggles by various groups to direct the power of the state to support their own interests. The element of truth in this point threatens to obscure a feature of the nation-state worth pondering as people decide how much of themselves to invest in the American national "we." The appeal to a common destiny—to a sense that we, as Americans, are all in it together—has been a vital element in the mobilization of state power on behalf of a number of worthy causes. The successes of the Civil Rights movement owed something to this intangible nationalism. "It was *the* United States, the American people—not just some of them," as historian David Farber has summarized the matter, that African Americans were able to hold responsible "for guaranteeing one standard of basic social provision, justice, and equality before the law."[17]

The building of the welfare state, too, was justified with reference to a sense of nationhood. The Progressive Movement and the New Deal and the Great Society, whatever else they may have been, were decidedly nationalist movements, claiming to speak on behalf of the American nation, just as the comparable welfare-state initiatives in other industrialized nation-states were predicated on national solidarity. Anyone who believes that a national interest was served by the commitment of the state to the welfare of its citizens—however imperfectly and inconsistently acted upon—may suspect that not all claims to a common, national interest are equally disingenuous. If the United States of the 1970s, 1980s, and 1990s had been possessed of a stronger sense of national solidarity, it is possible that agreeing upon a national system of health care would have proved less formidable a challenge for the American polity.

What the worldwide crisis of the nation-state has done to the United States is to place under renewed pressure a national solidarity that has always been episodic. One source of pressure is the diasporic consciousness that flourishes under the aegis of multiculturalism. This consciousness is guarded about the American nation because of its assimilationist potential, but it looks to the state as a source of entitlements. The second source of pressure on the American nation-state is considerably more portentous, but it gets insufficient attention in discussions of separatism. This is the opportunity that globalization presents for American capitalists to maintain and increase their profits without attention to the economic and social welfare of the nation. More and more of their employees live in Manila, Taipei, and the Dominican Republic. A business elite with a transnational focus will find certain uses for the American state, but it has little need for the nation. From the American national community, this business elite can, in some ways, separate itself. Those who worry about the fragmenting of America would do well to attend more closely to this variety of separatism.

The American nation, in the meantime, has not gone unattended. While diasporic consciousness and multinational corporations render the American nation less vital and immediate for Americans caught up in particularization and globalization, the nation is being claimed with increasingly fierce determination by a third constituency that proved its strength in the elections of 1994. A complex of movements and organizations commonly associated with Middle America and evangelical Christianity, and with the earnest defense of family values, are prominent elements in this third constituency. These people tend to be suspicious of the state, except as an enforcer of personal morality, but they believe, with a vengeance, in America. Their political heroes include Congressman Newt Gingrich of Georgia and the television and radio commentator Rush Limbaugh.[18]

These three constituencies are not the only players in the American drama of the nation's relation to the state. But all three are prominent in the cast of characters, and each helps to loosen the specific link between nation and state that facilitated the expansion of public responsibility for welfare and that responded to the Civil Rights movement. All three of these constituencies are the object of critical argumentation. Robert Reich, James Fallows, and others have tried to persuade the business elite of the importance of the nation.[19] Arguments to the effect that Middle Americans have too narrow a cultural sense of the American nation and too restricted a political sense of the American state are staples of multiculturalist discourse. Less easy to come by are arguments of the kind I am making in this chapter. I believe that proponents of diasporic consciousness have rather less to fear from the

American nation—and more to gain—than many of them appear to believe, and that the cosmopolitan element in multiculturalism is compatible with a strong affirmation of American nationality.

The terms in which Appadurai casts his obituary for the American nation-state exemplifies, once again, a position increasingly popular in multiculturalist circles, and thus invites critical appraisal here. The United States has generated "a powerful fable of itself as a land of immigrants," says Appadurai, who asserts that the old liberal ideas about American nationality simply cannot deal with the "thoroughly diasporic" realities presented by recent immigration. Appadurai urges attention to "the difference between being a land of immigrants and being one node in a postnational network of diasporas." The United States is "no longer a closed space for the melting pot to work its magic" but a place where "people come to seek their fortunes but are no longer content to leave their homelands behind." A suitable role for the United States is to serve as "a free trade zone for the generation, circulation, importation, and testing of the materials for a world organized around diasporic diversity." In this context, patriotism for the United States might well be replaced, or supplemented, by a series of "new sovereignties," of which "queer nation may be only the first," followed, perhaps, by "the retired, the unemployed, and the disabled, as well as scientists, women, and Hispanics."[20]

Appadurai exaggerates the novelty of the contemporary

conditions that inspire his observations. The history of the United States suggests that this nation-state is more equipped than most to cope with a world of simultaneously globalizing and particularizing forces. The vitality of immigrant communities early in the century, as measured by foreign-language newspapers and publishing houses, rendered the United States in the 1920s decidedly more multicultural than it is now. In the Polish language alone, sixty-seven weekly newspapers, eighteen monthlies, and nineteen dailies, the largest of which had a circulation of more than a hundred thousand, were regularly published in the United States in 1923. Moreover, approximately one-third of all the immigrants who came to the United States in the great migration of 1880 to 1924 actually returned to their country of origin. To take the Poles, once again, as an example: of the nearly one and a half million Polish immigrants between the turn of the century and 1924, nearly 40 percent went back to Poland.[21] Back-and-forth migration of foreign workers was the norm, not the exception. Appadurai is a victim of the common misconception that pre-1924 immigration differed greatly from post-1965 immigration in the timing and intensity of immigrant attachment to the United States.[22]

Students of today's diasporas and their relation to the American national community would do well to examine the earlier case of one of the European groups that eventually became part of the American mainstream: the Italians. More than *half* of the nearly four million people who entered the United States from Italy between 1899 and 1924 decided not stay. If the melting pot ever worked in the "closed space" invoked by Appadurai as the salient historical contrast to today's diasporas, it did so only during the 1924–1965 interregnum between migrations; even then it was affected by a culturally conspicuous migration from Hitler's Europe and by a steady stream of illegal immigrants from Mexico. The new immigration since 1965 is behaviorally mixed, like the old. It displays a variety of degrees of engagement with the United States and with prior homelands, and it yields some strong assimilationist impulses alongside vivid expressions of diasporic consciousness. Today's demography of immigration has its novelties, but uncertain attachment to the United States is not one of them.

The fundamental difference between the two immigrations is not that one was assimilationist and the other diasporic; rather, the economic conditions have changed.[23] The opportunities in a highly controlled, service-oriented economy are narrower than in the expanding, production-oriented economy of the earlier era of massive immigration. There are additional differences between the two great migrations, but most of them render the American nation-state more important, not less, to the lives of immigrant workers than it was in 1890 or 1910. In the era of free immigration it was easier for foreign workers to move in and out of the United States at will than it is today; now, movement is more tightly regulated. Today's immigrants are more prepared for a measure of assimilation by the worldwide influence of American popular culture; most are more culturally attuned to the United States before they arrive here than were their counterparts of a century ago. More importantly, immigrant communities are also acculturated into a vastly different political atmosphere. "Unlike the political institutions in place during the last great wave of immigration," observes Peter Skerry, "those in place today" encourage immigrants "to define themselves as a victimized group that cannot advance without the help of racially assigned benefits" derived from the state.[24]

Appadurai's vision of America as home to an expanse of particularist affiliations, too, is more traditional than he seems to realize. The assertion of group identities is so mainstream an activity that it is often observed that to affirm such subnational identities is an American ritual. The assertion of subnational particularisms is a well-established mode of finding one's way within American society. So pronounced is this tendency in American life that even Anglo-Protestants, when they find themselves "alone," will often make a production out of dividing themselves into places of origin. The "All-States Picnic" of Southern California in the middle decades of this century, for example, reproduced trivially the clustering by ethno-racial groups taking place in the society at large: everyone was "from" Iowa, or Oklahoma, or some other state whose migrants to California had their own organization to plan each year's picnic—a set of tables for each state-ethnos—and to build that state's float for the big parade down Ontario's Euclid Avenue.

Organized interest groups, moreover, have long been a staple of American public life, and in exactly the categories listed by Appadurai: the retired, women, ethno-racial groups, and trade and professional associations. The proliferation of voluntary associations in the United States has been a staple of commentary on American society since Tocqueville. Some of these affiliations were decidedly transnational, like the vast movement in support of Christian missions abroad associated with missionary organizations of western Europe. Today, the American Association of Retired Persons, an organization of thirty-three million dues-paying members, seems able to handle its dual loyalties—to the aged and to the nation—rather comfortably. Whether it makes sense to call Queer Nation and the AARP sovereignties is dubious, however, and may exaggerate their power.[25]

We might bring these affiliations down to political earth, and enable them to find a place within postethnic nationality, if we instead understood these various and shifting affiliations as publics nested within a larger public that is the polity of the United States. "The concept of a public," philosopher Nancy Fraser points out, "presupposes a plurality of perspectives among those who participate within it, thereby allowing for internal differences and antagonisms, and likewise discouraging reified blocs." In this view, the affiliations to which Appadurai alludes can be arenas for the formation of culture and for deliberation and argumentation concerning matters at issue in the larger, national public as well as internal to a given community. As an example, Fraser invokes "the late-twentieth-century U.S. feminist subaltern counterpublic," which, through "its variegated array of journals, bookstores, publishing companies, film and video distribution networks, lecture series, research centers, academic programs, conferences, conventions, festivals, and local meeting places" has affected the life of the larger American public.[26]

It is the reality, integrity, and positive value of this larger American public that celebrants of multiple publics and of diasporic solidarities are sometimes slow to appreciate. They treat common ground not as a commitment to one another within which we negotiate a future across the lines of acknowledged and respected difference, the way juries work toward a common verdict without pretending to collapse the differences they bring to the task;[27] rather, common ground is feared as a trick to hoodwink some Americans into sacrificing their interests for someone else's interests disguised as a common interest. Against this pathological fear of the common, Sheldon Wolin has warned that "heterogeneity, diversity [and] multiple selves are no match for modern forms of power." We need, Wolin adds, to look beyond "multicultural politics" and "localism" toward "the evanescent homogeneity" of a broader polity.[28]

Americans have become too afraid of each other, and too unwilling to take up the task of building a common future. Part of the problem is with the notion "common," which when coupled with "ground" is often taken rather preciously to imply a uniform opinion on whatever questions are at issue. But "to be linked in a common fate," Kathleen Sullivan rightly points out, "is not the same as applying collective will to a common project."[29] The national community's fate can be common without its will being uniform, and the nation can constitute a common project without effacing all of the various projects that its citizens pursue through their voluntary affiliations.

But a theme in multiculturalist discourse has been the discrediting, as nationalist, of efforts to identify cultural adhesives that enable Americans to feel a sense of peoplehood while continuing to recognize their own diversity. Historians and literary scholars who construct narratives of the people of the United States and of the literature or political ideas created by Americans are frequently accused of carrying out projects in the service not of any people but rather of the state.[30] Chasing down and exposing as reactionary those who try to address the question of the national culture has become a popular search-and-destroy sport. A luminous example is a vitriolic attack launched by Barbara Herrnstein Smith, a recent president of the Modern Language Association, against E. D. Hirsch's project of "cultural literacy."

One need have no special sympathy for Hirsch's list of facts that Americans should know to be struck by the ferocity of Smith's determination to convict Hirsch of not wanting children "to identify, as their own community, any social unit either smaller, larger, or other than the *nation*." She depicts the United States as a panorama of "communities" and "cultures," and mocks the "national culture" as "media hype and 4th of July speeches." Smith displays no sense that amid the diversity of the United States, there might be any value to a sense of national solidarity. Although Smith writes in the voice of a stylized, tough realism against Hirsch's no doubt excessive hopes for what a list of facts can do for the poor, it is not clear which of the two is the more naive. Rather than engage the more difficult task of deciding what basic points of reference it might be useful for Americans to share and what mechanisms might promote such a goal, Smith simply laughs Hirsch out of the conversation as a patriotic fool:

> Wild applause; fireworks; music—*America the Beautiful*; all together, now: *Calvin Coolidge, Gunga Din, Peter Pan, spontaneous combustion.* Hurrah for America and the national culture! Hurrah![31]

It is doubtful that Smith would similarly parody the educational programs associated with Black History Month, where basic facts about the accomplishments of African Americans are made accessible. Were she to do so, it might sound like this:

> Wild applause; fireworks; music—*We Shall Overcome;* all together, now: *Father Divine, Ralph Bunche, Chicago Blues, the NAACP, double consciousness.* Hurrah, hurrah, for the African American culture! Hurrah!

What is at issue for Smith is not the rudimentary devices by which young people can learn something about the solidarities with which their elders wish them to be affiliated or with which they want them to be familiar. At issue, rather, is one such solidarity, America, and how much or how little cultural content it should be understood to have.

From a postethnic perspective, the United States certainly can and should be a setting for the development of a great number of voluntary associations of many different sorts, including transnational affiliations. But there is no valid cause for surprise or dismay if these transnational affiliations take on an American aspect. "Even if the aim of associational life is to sustain difference," Michael Walzer has wisely observed in the course of an eloquent case for the desirability of robust voluntary associations in the United States,

> that aim has to be achieved *here,* under American conditions, and the result is commonly a new and

unintended kind of differentiation—of American
Catholics and Jews, say, not so much from one
another or from the Protestant majority as from
Catholics and Jews in other cultures.[32]

The temptation to regard the United States as merely a
container of cultures that come and go rather than as a cultural entity in itself should be examined in specific relation
to some of the lessons learned during the age of ethnos-
consciousness we have just experienced. If people do need
to belong, and if there is no escaping the drawing of boundaries, these insights can apply to the national community of
the United States as well as to more global and to more
local solidarities. If all solidarities are ultimately constructs,
and not primordial, it will not do to pronounce as artificial
the cultural continuities that have developed in relation to
the American nation-state, and to then take at face value
the claims to authenticity made on behalf of other cultures.
Indeed, the distinction between civic and ethnic eventually
breaks down because over the course of time civic affiliations can help to create those that are eventually recognized as ethnic.

American nationality certainly needs to be demystified,
but we should keep alive our ability to demystify the other
nationalities and protonationalities whose claims are now
routinely advanced against a hegemonic American culture.
One need not believe in an American genius to contemplate

the actual history of cultural creativity that has taken place within the United States over the course of the last two hundred years, stimulated not only by an Anglo-Protestant heritage but by a diversity of other sources. The history that has led so many citizens of the United States to call themselves Americans is just as real as is the history that yields the identities brought here amid diasporas.

A measure of historical particularity can help to save the United States from the illusion that it is a proto-world-state. This, too, is a lesson of the ethnos-consciousness of the past generation. The United States will fall well short of its potential as an agent of democratic-egalitarian values if it tries to stretch itself to accommodate on the same terms every diaspora, every claim to group rights, every set of taboos and inhibitions that demand respect in the name of diversity. Rather, it makes more historical and practical sense for the United States to maintain its own public culture—constantly contested and critically revised, to be sure—against which the demands of various particularisms shall be obliged to struggle within a formal constitutional framework. The United States should not try to be all things to all people. We can even be a people, so long as we remember that we are not a chosen people, or even the "almost chosen people" invoked by Lincoln, but merely a people among peoples, in the sense that Geertz urged a modest "we" understood as "a case among cases, a world among worlds."[33]

The Americanizers of the early twentieth-century were

clearly wrong to have tried to make America into a mono-lithic culture. Horace Kallen made an equally conservative mistake in the opposite direction by wanting to reduce the United States to an administrative canopy under which a variety of old-world clans could perpetuate themselves. Both resisted novelty. Both, like their less extreme successors on today's middle-American Right and today's multi-culturalist Left, tried to resolve the old American problem of "the one and the many" by relaxing it, by pushing toward either "one" or "many." A postethnic perspective is willing to live with this problem and to treat it as an opportunity rather than try to escape from it.

A postethnic perspective invites critical engagement with the United States as a distinctive locus of social identity mediating between the human species and its varieties, and as a vital arena for political struggles the outcome of which determine the domestic and global use of a unique concentration of power. Such an engage-ment with the American nation need not preclude other engagements, including affiliations of varying intensity and duration defined by material or imagined consan-guinity. A virtue of the term *post*ethnic is to distinguish the perspective on American nationality sketched here from any reversion to a *pre*ethnic perspective on that nationality, according to which the general question of the ethnos is dismissed rather than critically addressed and the specific issue of ethno-racial identity is suppressed by a monolithic, "100 percenter" notion of American citizenship. Being an American amid a multiplicity of affiliations need not be dangerously threatening to diversity. Nor need it be too shallow to constitute an important solidarity of its own.

EPILOGUE

No industrialized nation has so large a percentage of its population in prison as does the United States. And no such nation is producing so many mixed-race people. These two facts about the United States are not directly related. Yet they bear mention together because of the antithetical implications these two realities have for a postethnic America. The extraordinary increase in marriage and reproduction across the lines of the ethno-racial pentagon presents a fundamental challenge to the authority of descent-defined categories. A critical mass of acknowledged mixed-race people heightens the credibility of an ideal according to which individuals decide how tightly or loosely they wish to affiliate with one or more communities of descent. These Americans help move the society in a postethnic direction. In the meantime, the imprisoning of more and more of the population is an emblem for a complex of social and economic conditions that obstruct postethnicity and feed the suspicion that the United States is in the process of squandering whatever opportunity it may now have to become more postethnic.

Mixed-race people are a powerful symbol for an opportunity long said to distinguish American society from that of most societies in Europe and Asia: the making of new affiliations. If this willingness to forge new communities and new cultural combinations has often been limited by racism, this willingness is nonetheless a common theme in American folklore, popular ideology, and law. Legal scholar Robert Post has pointed out that an important "function of law" according to much of American constitutional adjudication "is to protect the capacity of individuals to form new and different groups." By contrast, British courts are more likely to assume that the law's function in relation to cultural diversity is rather to "protect the integrity of established and stable groups" within "a stable and established social fabric."[1] Mixed-race people are performing a historic role at the present moment: they are reanimating a traditional American emphasis on the freedom of individual affiliation, and they are confronting the American nation with its own continued reluctance to apply this principle to ethno-racial affiliations.

In the meantime, the number of prisons and prisoners grows. To the extent that the young people going off to prison are African Americans—which in our cities of today, they often are—these time-servers perpetuate the very low-class position associated with their group and thus keep alive the debate over whether it is class or race that steers them toward prison. Economic and educational opportunities do not guarantee that members of historically disadvantaged ethno-racial groups will attain the standard of living associated with the middle class, nor even that they will avoid prison. But these economic and educational opportunities do provide the crucial occasions for members of such groups to *test* the social and cultural barriers that have traditionally disadvantaged them. Too few African Americans, especially, get enough of these occasions to actually test the strength of the prejudice against them. Asian Americans, who as a group possess a higher class position, get more such opportunities, and with results that are often encouraging. The disadvantages of class and of race are deeply entangled in history, but the chances of diminishing racial inequalities are now limited by obvious class inequalities.

Arguments will continue to rage over how racist this society is and over the extent to which the degraded conditions experienced in American cities can be attributed ultimately to racism. But a society that will not take steps to help its poor citizens of all ethno-racial groups will have little chance to find out how successful have been its efforts to overcome the racist attitudes of empowered whites. The more inflexible the class structure, the longer will the ethno-racial groups caught in its lower segments remain there. The members of these groups will find it harder to hope for a middle-class existence and will have more and more reason to interpret as structural or institutional racism those policies that, even if devoid of prejudicial intent, have a disproportionately negative impact on them. Meanwhile, the prejudiced attitudes of some members of more prosperous groups will be reinforced by what they take to be evidence of the criminality of "other races."

These realities about race and class in America are too well known to bear elaboration here. I mention them simply to underscore the obstacles they place in the way of a postethnic America. In the absence of a more ambitious national program for enabling poor people to find their way out of poverty and attendant suffering, ethno-racial particularism will flourish. Ethno-racial affiliations can be vital even to people experiencing prosperity; these solidarities can be truly precious to people who lack opportunities for forming other sustaining communities. Critics who simply denounce separatism and call upon ethno-racial minorities to "just say no" would do well to focus more attention on the rigidification of the class structure. Glenn Loury persuasively argues that the merely "tenuous" commitment of the United States "to providing for the poor of any race" creates an "ideological trap" for African American leaders and intellectuals who "think they must emphasize black victimization because it provides the only secure basis for pressing claims on behalf of their most disadvantaged fellows."[2] The most compelling historian of America's poor, Jacqueline Jones, sees this trap, and warns that for African Americans to "identify one's interests on the basis of skin color is to continue to shoulder the burden of slavery." A "politics based on race" is "self-defeating" for poor blacks and whites alike, Jones observes, in a society in which there are twice as many whites as blacks below the poverty line.[3]

I do not pretend to know how strong or how weak are the forces that stand in the way of a more postethnic America. Just how deep is the racism of whites, and how desperate is the situation of ethno-racial minorities, especially African Americans? This question has been the basis for a diverting contest to see who can be the most hard-boiled about America and who can flee the most convincingly from the notion that the United States is one big, happy family. In our shared frustration over a rate of progress much slower than any of us want, we too often yield to the game of competitive disillusionment, and are quick to accuse one another of being too optimistic. "Don't you realize," we say to each other, "that children are being shot in the schools of Los Angeles and Detroit," as though this fact somehow renders silly another person's modest effort to identify and exploit what resources the nation may have to diminish its problems. So, while many of these problems worsen, we can congratulate ourselves on our tough-mindedness: life may be hell in Los Angeles's South Central neighborhood, but at least we are under no illusions about it. While remaining uncertain about what programs might actually work, we can derive some compensatory satisfaction from beating up verbally on those who do not signal their despair with sufficient conviction.

In this book, I have tried not to play this tempting game. I take for granted that the economic, political, and cultural obstacles to a postethnic America are truly formidable, but I also take for granted that revulsion against ethno-racial prejudice is strong enough in the United States today to render the ideal of postethnicity worth developing. We may never have a postethnic America. But whatever chances there may be for such a consummation will amount to nothing if the ideal is not articulated and defended.

Our generation is perhaps unprecedented in the brilliance with which it spews forth good arguments for drawing boundaries and for emphasizing the differences between people. To recognize this virtue in ourselves may render us more critical in its exercise and may better enable us to facilitate what we might call the Edwin Markham effect, inspired by the turn-of-the-century poet most remembered for having demanded the inclusion into "our circle" of "The Man with the Hoe":

He drew a circle that shut me out—
Heretic, rebel, a thing to flout.

But Love and I had the wit to win:
We drew a circle that took him in![4]

These hopeful lines of Edwin Markham, once standard reading in eighth-grade English, celebrate a process by which persons who have been excluded end up helping to redraw the circles that enclose. The entry of women into the leadership of civic, moral, and epistemic communities is a salient example of this Edwin Markham effect now in process, with an extent and significance still to be determined. The gradual, episodic entry of various, specific entho-racial minorities into the leadership of the United States is another. The politics that produce this effect are a good bit more complicated than the "love" invoked by the old progressive poet. But if this great sentiment can be construed as a concern for the welfare of a community larger than that of the excluded group seeking entry, it has often been a vital force in the process. This was the case in the Civil Rights movement as led by Martin Luther King, Jr., which affirmed a national American "we" and the solidarity of black people at the same time.

The basic character of the Edwin Markham effect was understood and appreciated by Henry James, Markham's more diffident and divided contemporary. Even in 1907, when so many Anglo-Protestants of James's milieu feared being dispossessed of their country by "aliens," James depicted the immigrant dispossessors as fully "at home" in

America, and called upon his own tribe to partially "surrender" to the authority of the new. "We must go . . . *more*
than half-way to meet them," James insisted, asking that
Anglo-Protestants of long American lineage see their own
future as indissolubly bound up with the children of these
immigrants, who "are the stuff of which brothers and sisters
are made." James confessed to some nostalgia for the old,
homogeneous "idea of country," but rather than follow the
"instinct . . . of keeping the idea simple and strong and continuous" he instead demanded that "we, not they, must
make the surrender." And "they" are no more the "alien,"
and no less the "American," James declared, than are "we."[5]
They can no longer be cut out of the circle because they
have begun to draw it, as well they should.

But not all exclusions are bad, the conventional wisdom
of our time will be quick to remind anyone who looks too
uncritically on the Edwin Markham effect. Boundaries are
necessary. A postethnic perspective understands this.
Which boundaries, and where? We are all left with the
responsibility for deciding where to try to draw what circles
with whom, and around what.

Culture, Color, and Solidarity

"You have written the wrong book for the times," a friend said to me shortly after this book was published in 1995, "because you don't attack anybody, and you are too reasonable." But the debate over multiculturalism changed rapidly during the next five years. Stridency diminished when the initial, indignant polemics reached the point of diminishing returns in dealing with issues that resisted quick closure. Quarrels over the pros and cons of "identity politics" were largely replaced by more far-reaching discussions of cosmopolitanism, nationalism, globalization, diasporas, the concept of race, and the legal rights of cultural minorities. The number of people deserving attack no doubt remains substantial, and the limits of reason remain as formidable as ever. But I offer this postscript in the belief that *Postethnic America* speaks better to the enduring aspects of the multiculturalist controversy than to the preoccupations of most discussants in the early 1990s.

Between 1995 and 2000 the conversation moved toward, rather than away from, several of the concerns that most separated *Postethnic America* from the bulk of writings about multiculturalism that were current when it was first published. Prominent among these concerns are ethno-racial mixture, color's relation to culture, the character of American nationalism, the rigidification of the class structure, and the relation of the ethno-racially diverse United States to the political demography of an economically integrated but unequal world. A decline in invective has led to reports that the culture wars are over. These reports reflect the press's boredom with public arguments that do not take the form of shootouts. The multiculturalist controversy still flourishes in the nation's schools, colleges, and universities, and in the discourse of political scientists, historians, literary scholars, sociologists, anthropologists, philosophers, and specialists in ethnic and religious studies. Thanks to the work of these scholars,[1] the critical discussion of the United States in relation to diasporic cultures, global migrations, and international economic integration is more sharply defined and more intellectually demanding in 2000 than five years before. The debate has gained in importance as it has moved in these directions. More and more people recognize the depth and durability of the issues now being debated.

Deep and durable too are several sentiments that *Postethnic America* challenges. One of these is the sense that color and culture, for all their claims to independence, really do belong together after all. My argument that our society would be much better off organizing our appreciation of cultural diversity on a

basis different from that on which our antidiscrimination remedies are organized seems to some readers to ignore a natural connection. A second deeply rooted sentiment challenged by this
book is that the ideal of individual choice, appropriate as it is for
many areas of life, does not apply well to matters of identity. My
insistence that ethno-racial affiliation ought to be more voluntary
than ascribed has made some readers uncomfortable. A third feeling put on the defensive by this book is that the national community of the United States is too burdened with a history of racist
evil to play more than a marginal role in a struggle against racism,
which is better led by transnational and subnational solidarities.
My treatment of the American nation as a potential instrument
for advancing transnational, egalitarian goals has led some readers to find me insufficiently cynical about the United States.

This postscript deals directly with these three points of tension between the book and the dispositions brought to it by some
potentially sympathetic readers. I expand arguments made in the
chapters and introduce some additional points that take account
of recent developments within the United States and the world.[2]
Although the emphasis is on points of some contention, I do not
want to leave the impression that the general reception of *Postethnic America* has been hostile. Far from it. I simply want to engage
the critical discussion of the book in ways that can clarify and
strengthen the perspective it advances.

But before I take up these tasks, I am obliged to acknowledge
that almost immediately after the book was first published my
treatment of affirmative action was rendered out of date by an
unexpected turn of events. Affirmative action, the continued exis-

tence of which I had taken for granted, was virtually eliminated in California. The voters of the state acted against it by passing Proposition 209, and the Regents of the University of California, anticipating this action, moved on their own authority to ban affirmative action in the university. Although this turn of events was specific to California, it had national implications. And California is not the only state in which legislation or court rulings have now diminished programs entailing group preferences for ethno-racial minorities. Quickly, I supplemented the book with an article, "Group Preferences, Cultural Diversity, and Social Democracy: Notes Toward a Theory of Affirmative Action," explaining the political failure of affirmative action partly in terms of the inability of its defenders to agree upon just what it is, why it is needed, and what groups should be included in it.[3] But the matter demands attention here as well.

I want to underscore my belief that the historically unique experience of black people in the United States justifies a continuing effort to design programs of educational and employment opportunity that can mitigate the effects of slavery and Jim Crow. Such programs are best defended as exceptional and temporary expedients along the way toward a society in which individuals will be treated equally regardless of ascribed or asserted ethno-racial identities. In the case of black Americans, the circumstances justify the risk of perpetuating a color line the invidiousness of which a postethnic perspective is designed to diminish.[4] What are these justifying circumstances?

Within the population of the United States today, blacks are the only ethno-racial group to inherit a *multicentury legacy of group-specific enslavement and extensive, institutionalized debasement under the ordinance of federal constitutional authority.* Indians also have a strong claim for special treatment, but the legal standing of tribes as sovereign entities invites, and indeed provides the basis for, a differently configured response to the historic mistreatment of Indians. A measure of the difference between the legacies of these two cases of white racist aggression, moreover, is found in the strikingly contrasting images these two minorities generate in popular imagination today. During the last several decades many white Americans have discovered and trumpeted their Indian ancestry, while eagerness to move into the black segment of the ethno-racial pentagon remains, if not negligible, considerably less widespread. The ease with which persons of some Indian ancestry are able to move back and forth between white and Indian worlds contrasts with the continued operation of the one-drop rule, by which persons of the slightest perceptible trace of black ancestry are treated as black. This does not diminish the iniquity of what whites did to the continent's indigenous population under the authority of the United States, nor does it diminish the obligation of the nation to address it. But the distinction does lend credibility to the idea, supported by numerous sociological studies of the class position of the bulk of African Americans—35 percent of black children live in poverty—that blackness and the heritage of slavery and Jim Crow together constitute a unique obstacle to economic and social achievement. I hope that the effort to design programs that can pass constitutional muster will continue. Had affirmative action for black people been so seriously threatened before 1995, I would have said all this very plainly at that time.

Reference to affirmative action and its theoretical justification brings me directly to the first of the three points of tension that focus this postscript.

Postethnic America contends that the politics of culture and the politics of color have become too entangled with one another, and they get in each other's way. Specifically, I argue that antidiscrimination remedies, including affirmative action, and the appreciation of cultural diversity, including academic programs in multiculturalism, can best achieve their aims if they go their own separate ways. This contention cuts against the grain of the widespread sense that color and culture have a natural intimacy. I faulted the multiculturalist movement for treating the traditional color distinctions (black, yellow, white, red, and brown) as cultural distinctions: African American, Asian American, European American, Indian, and Latino. This practice, I observed, reproduced "the most gross and invidious of popular images of what makes human beings different from one another" (32). Culture is much more diverse than these categories imply, I argued. Not only are French, Chinese, Jewish, Korean, Zuni, and Irish more culture-specific terms than European American, Asian American, and so on, but culture is also manifest in religious, national, and other communities that are not ethno-racially defined. Antidiscrimination remedies, by contrast, are appropriately color-centered. These remedies are designed to deal with the discriminatory acts triggered primarily by the physical marks of descent, especially skin color.

"Culture *is* blood," retorted a representative of an American Indian political organization in the midst of a televised debate he and I had in San Francisco shortly after this book was published. So overbearingly biocentric an understanding of culture retains few adherents these days in the United States. But my suggestion that without color the ethno-racial pentagon makes little sense has unnerved even some people who have forsaken biology for ostensibly more enlightened cultural understandings of race and ethnicity. One place where we see in full flower the presumption that culture and color go together is the controversy over the federal census. I alluded to this in several chapters, but I want to address this particular controversy in more detail because it reveals the pitfalls of conflating color with culture.

Most advocates of a mixed-race classification are looking for a way to affirm a cultural orientation not exclusively white or black or defined by any other single color. Their mixture is just as real as the specific color-coded ancestries that they are constantly being asked to declare. Tired of having to suppress their true cultural identities, mixed-descent advocates demand recognition through the census. Meanwhile, opponents of a mixed-race classification insist that if people of mixed descent opt out of their popularly understood color category, the government will lack accurate counts relevant to antidiscrimination remedies. It will then be harder to protect the rights of people who have been historically discriminated against in voting, education, and employment as a result of the physical marks of race. In this view, the counting of people by color-marked communities of descent is justified because society has an interest in antidiscrimination remedies that depend on numbers.

Both sides in this dispute are basically right. Classifying people by color makes good sense if the point is to identify people according to the physical characteristics that render them the most vulnerable to mistreatment. In the struggle against discrimination, mixture matters little. What counts is the degree of non-whiteness sufficient to mark an individual as a member of a stigmatized bloc. In some situations the Anglophilic writer of Mexican American descent Richard Rodriguez will be no less subject to abuse than a new immigrant from Guatemala or a leader of a Chicano nationalist organization. If what is being classified is cultural, on the other hand, the case for using the pentagonal categories is weak. An individual who has every right to protection against discrimination on the basis of his or her involuntary classification as a member of a historically disadvantaged color group may have no interest whatsoever in the culture popularly associated with that group.

But the two sides to the census debate have proven lamentably slow to join issue over exactly what is being mixed, with what significance, and where the mixture must be displayed. As a result of their dodging of these vital issues, they tragically hold each other's virtues hostage. The root of the problem is the failure to distinguish color from culture. So long as a single census question is used, and so long as the census is understood to be a register of cultural as well as color identity, the stalemate will continue. The United States Congress has done little to help. By approving for the 2000 census the option of an individual's being classified in more than one category, the government has continued to keep the issue fuzzy. Early reports on the public's response to Census 2000 indicates that most people continue to believe that the census is expected to register cultural identity as well as color group.

What might the Census Bureau do? It might find a way to solicit information about color and about culture, but not with a single question. It might ask, in effect, Do you have the physical characteristics that render you at risk of discrimination, and if so, do those characteristics make you black, red, yellow, or brown? This question—too cumbersome as worded here for practical use—speaks exactly to the justified concern of opponents of the mixed-race category. Many mixed-descent individuals, moreover, could easily answer yes without violating their cultural identity, and could specify the color according to which they are the most at risk of mistreatment. Their cultural identity could be registered by answering a second cumbersome question, Do you consider yourself to be a member of any of the following ethno-racially defined cultural groups? This could be asked in relation to a list of ethno-racial categories including various specific mixtures, and might provide the opportunity to write in any identity not listed. Tiger Woods, the professional golfer almost as famous for his mixture of descent as for his string of tournament victories, can describe himself as he wishes in response to this second question. But a census official would have reason to quibble if Woods, in answer to the earlier question about physical characteristics, denied that he should be classified as black.

The relation of color to culture is thus best seen as context-specific. If color-blindness will not do across the board in public policy because it stands in the way of much-needed antidiscrimination remedies, color-consciousness will not do across the board either. It stands in the way of an appreciation of the full span of cultural diversity and threatens to keep individuals imprisoned in color-coded boxes.

It is against this programmed destiny that mixed-descent activists justifiably struggle. It is easy to fault them for expecting the census to offer a legitimization better sought elsewhere. But these activists work within a widespread understanding of ethno-racial categories that is not their creation. Recognizing how that understanding was fostered and reinforced may help us appreciate the historical contingency of the conventions that now govern the national conversation about race and ethnicity, and thus enable us to escape from their thrall. It is to this bit of recent history that I now turn.

The central event in the story is the *Bakke* case of 1978. Culture was tightly linked to color-coded descent communities when Supreme Court justice Lewis Powell, struggling for a way to justify preferences in academic admissions for historically disadvantaged ethno-racial minorities, declared such preferences potentially permissible if their aim was to diversify the "ideas and mores" of campuses. Powell was part of the five-justice majority that invalidated the affirmative action program of the medical school at the University of California at Davis on the grounds that the program's setting aside of places for nonwhites violated Title VI of the Civil Rights Act of 1964. This provision of federal law prohibited the use of race, Powell and his colleagues concluded in *Bakke,* as a basis for deciding who could or could not participate in a federally funded program. But Powell, in a paragraph that became the constitutional foundation for affirmative action programs in higher education, went on to distinguish group preferences as such from group preferences in their capacity as instruments of cultural diversification. The ethno-racial status of an individual could be taken into account amid other considerations, Powell said, in the interest of achieving a diverse campus environment. Powell explained that the nation's future depended on leaders exposed to "ideas and mores . . . as diverse as this Nation of many peoples."[5]

Powell's device for saving group preferences from the nation's egalitarian principles would not have worked as well as it did for two decades had it not embodied a large measure of easily recognized truth about the relation of color to culture. The overwhelming majority of people within each of the four nonwhite categories named in the Davis program—"Blacks," "Chicanos," "Asians," and "American Indians"—had been subject, directly or indirectly, to racist conditions that endowed them with life experiences different from those of the average white person. The cultural life of all Americans, including empowered whites, obviously derived in part from the operation of a color hierarchy of long standing, the ordinance of which over particular groups had increased or decreased in specific locales at different times. The customs, tastes, and values that came to be stereotypically associated with each ethno-racial group had been affected, moreover, not only by the unequal distribution of power and prestige among such groups but also by distinctive historical matrices made up of a variety of languages, religious orientations, and points of geographic origin. The mantra that race is constituted by culture as well as color may be misleading, but it is not altogether false. Powell's formulations gained additional credibility from a popular and enduring presumption in the North Atlantic west that what Powell called ideas and mores were largely ethno-racial phenomena in any case. If this presumption was somewhat discredited by its extreme development in Nazi cultural doctrine and practice, the presumption, in more benign forms—such as my Indian interlocutor's assertion that culture is blood—has not disappeared.

Yet the presumption of an ethno-racial basis for culture—that ideas and mores follow blood lines—was increasingly on the defensive in the United States between World War II and the 1970s, rendering Powell's reassertion of it in a progressive cause ironic. The Immigration and Nationality Act of 1965 eliminated the restrictions on immigration that had been enacted in 1924 on the basis of the blatantly racist belief that the distinctive "ideas and mores" of Asians and of Southern and Eastern Europeans made it impossible for such people to become part of a democratic, humane society. The children of pre-1924 immigrants had in fact achieved a high degree of structural assimilation in a society increasingly willing to call itself "a nation of immigrants," even though this term left out of account the segments of the population incorporated through enslavement and conquest. The massive intellectual attack on racism carried out by anthropologists, biologists, historians, sociologists, and other scholars from Gunnar Myrdal onward cut to ribbons the old doctrinal fabric in which communities of biological descent were woven together with necessary cultural consequences. These antiracist scholars disseminated the knowledge that the genes producing skin color and morphological traits did not generate the habits, attitudes, and dispositions stereotypically associated with the standardized ethno-racial groups. The Civil Rights movement of the 1950s and 1960s was directed, in part, against the notion that Negroes were burdened with race-specific social traits that prevented successful integration. The bulk of the government's antidiscrimination remedies, including the affirmative action programs developed during the administrations of Presidents Lyndon Johnson, Richard Nixon, and Gerald Ford, were designed to help not culture-bearing communities, but individuals whose physical appearance put them at risk of mistreatment or who inherited a legacy of mistreatment suffered by their ancestors. *It was thus possible to be "color-conscious" rather than "color-blind" in public affairs without assuming that persons of a given color were possessed of a particular culture.*

To be sure, a highly publicized upsurge of interest in ethnic cultures took place during the decade prior to *Bakke*. Yet the ethnic enthusiasms of the early and mid-1970s were not as color-coded as were those of the 1980s and 1990s. The new ethnic consciousness of the 1970s was most energetically displayed by segments of the white population celebrating Polish, Italian, Irish, Jewish, and other ethnicities. They did so in antiphonal relation to the celebration of black culture that had become conspicuous by the end of the 1960s. Hence the exaltations of cultural diversity and the attacks on melting-pot-style assimilation most prominent in the years immediately preceding *Bakke* did not automatically follow the logic of affirmative action. According to that logic, the cultural distinctions within the white population were beside the point. Before *Bakke* the appreciation for cultural diversity and the development of affirmative action programs were obviously grounded in some of the same political impulses, but the two proceeded in greater independence from one another than they did after *Bakke*.

It was during the 1980s, in the wake of Powell's language, that culture and color were more closely associated. Organizers of the movement to appreciate cultural diversity relied increasingly on the categories used in affirmative action programs sustained by courts following Powell's lead. These programs rightly focused on nonwhite groups identified largely by physical characteristics that had historically triggered prejudicial treatment at the hands of whites. There were excellent reasons for focusing on the cultures popularly associated with these nonwhite groups. The cultural creativity of nonwhites had indeed been given insufficient attention in American education and public discussion. Multicultural efforts to correct these omissions were magnificently successful, as measured by textbooks, anthologies, curricula, and the picture of American life displayed in the popular media. Especially did multiculturalism succeed in reinforcing and winning more widespread respect for an African American culture developed over many generations under conditions imposed by traditional, racist understandings of the color line. Multiculturalism's alliance with affirmative action also served symbolically to welcome nonwhites in new places; multiculturalism tried to provide schools, colleges, and universities with an environment that nonwhites, whatever their individual values and tastes, could see was intended as a warm response to their presence.

Yet this alliance had other, less happy effects. It narrowed into distinctly color-coded categories the revision, already under way in the 1960s and 1970s, of the nation's cultural self-conception from a predominantly Anglo-Protestant, masculinist one into a self-image more responsive to many different kinds of diversity. The alliance with affirmative action interrupted the demanding struggle to liberate culture from blood and soil in the interest of maximizing the opportunities of every individual to affiliate culturally as he or she might choose. It also left the impression that culture was more prominently at issue than it truly was in the dynamics of American racism. "It is not black culture that the racist hates," Anthony Appiah has put it bluntly, "but blacks."[6]

Powell treated color as a predictor of culture, and the multiculturalist movement largely followed suit. The notion that color and culture went naturally together was not invented by American multiculturalists or by Powell. It is an old staple of racialist thinking. But the multiculturalism of the 1980s and 1990s might not have been so thoroughly organized around the ethno-racial pentagon were it not for the turning of affirmative action toward a cultural justification after the *Bakke* case of 1978. Recognizing the expedient character of Powell's act, and of multiculturalism's use of color codes, may save us from mistaking a tactic for a truth.

The more room that culture is given to develop independently from the physical characteristics of individuals, the less power that race will have to control individual lives. Hence the question of color's relation to culture is closely linked to the question of how much choice individuals have in achieving those parts of their identities that imply affiliation with this or that

group. This brings me to the second of the deeply rooted sentiments challenged by *Postethnic America*, the feeling that individual choice, while a valuable goal in other contexts, is not so
important in matters of identity.

In the United States today identity, whatever else it may be, is a
zone of disputation within which various claims concerning an
individual's social character and obligations press against each
other. At issue, ultimately, is the distribution of solidarity. Identity is understood to be performative and social: one's identity
carries implications for the distribution of one's affections and
resources and energies, and for the claims one can make on the
affections and resources and energies of others. This is why I observed in the introduction to this book that when people in our
time talk about identities, they usually mean affiliations. I then
proceeded throughout the book to treat the two as synonyms,
and argued for the principle of affiliation by revocable consent.
This principle urges that we, as a society, encourage rather than
discourage individuals to make up their own minds about just
how much energy they put into their communities of descent.
Where the conditions for choice do not exist, as too often they
do not, *Postethnic America* urges that educational and public policy try to create conditions more conducive to choice. Yet this
emphasis on choice in the matter of affiliation has discomfited
some people, for whom the ostensibly nonchosen character of
identity is basic to its appeal. Recognition of the human need for
nonchosen imperatives is often taken, indeed, as the mark of a
profound mind.

Here I want to explain more deliberately the connection between identity and affiliation in the contemporary United States, and to argue more pointedly that the very link between identity and affiliation renders the social ideal of choice more, not less, appropriate.

Identity did not always mean group affiliation.[7] It once had to do primarily with psychological integration. In the heyday of Erik Erikson, identity was something a sound personality achieved, usually after a youthful crisis. The concept of identity applied to societies as a whole only when they were construed as analogs of an individual's personality or "character."[8] Some writers of the 1950s did analyze the national community of the United States in these terms. But this holistic style of analysis, often associated with "consensus history," was widely discredited in later decades. Throughout the 1980s and 1990s, however, a somewhat similar style of holistic analysis, under the sign of identity, came back into vogue when talking about ethno-racial communities. By then "American identity" was understood to be a shallow concept that masked diversity and implied a conformist mentality. But "Chicano identity" and "Asian American identity" and "black identity" were presented as deep concepts, in each case expressing a vital unity. Holism can thus wax and wane in relation to sentiments about just what wholes and parts are to be affirmed or denied. One party's whole can be another party's part, and vice-versa.

Identity became a way of establishing circles of "we" and "they." Who is in and who is out of the particular group that matters when identity is asserted or ascribed? This usage extends beyond ethno-racially defined collectivities. The movement for

"Catholic identity" is a means by which some colleges and universities of Catholic affiliation have sought to counteract the influence on campus culture of Protestants, Jews, and freethinkers. Even the University of Notre Dame, which has a strong Catholic identity movement of its own, finds itself accused by voices from other colleges of having failed to achieve and maintain a truly Catholic identity. And this effect is not limited to the United States. In the fall of 1999, citizens of the Dominican Republic trying to oust Haitians, to push them back across the border that divides the island they share, carried signs reading "Dominican Identity." It is no coincidence that the most far-out of the American religious right affiliations has taken for its name "Christian Identity."

Thus identity, whether understood as monolithic or multiple, enduring or contingent, has come to signify group affiliations entailing responsibilities. The concept of *solidarity* captures very well the implications that *identity* has come to carry along wherever it goes in contemporary American public discourse. That is why one can say that when people argue about identity, they are often arguing about the distribution of solidarity. Hence identity has taken on what we might call a political economy: it is a commodity distributed in one way or another on the basis of authority.

Once this is understood, a number of otherwise hidden issues concerning identity come out into the open. What is the authority by which claims about an individual's identity are warranted? To what extent does this authority reside in the will of the individual? If individual will is not a sufficiently authoritative basis for identity, who has the authority to ascribe identity to an individual, and what is the theoretical foundation for that authority? And on the basis of what considerations do these ascribers select, even to their own satisfaction, one identity rather than another to assign to a given person?

A striking feature of identity discourse in the United States is how rarely these questions are asked. What makes this noticeable is the fact that the country is filled with people who are quite willing to tell other folks what their identity is and isn't. Identity ascription flourishes best when no one asks hard questions about it. It is easier for the ascribers if no one challenges their authority or questions their principles of classification. The word *identity* still carries with it connotations of a given, natural order that enable claims and counterclaims about the distribution of solidarity to be advanced with a minimum of critical scrutiny. But the dynamics of solidarity distribution become clearer if we consider a certain class of contests over identity: those in which an individual declares an identity at variance with prevailing expectations.

An "African American" or an "Asian American" might self-identify as "white," or simply as "an American," or perhaps as "a Christian." Or a person we think of as white suddenly announces that he or she is Osage or Cherokee. We, as a society, generally resist such declarations, or trivialize them as subsidiary, on the authority of the physical evidence of skin color and morphological traits and the historical evidence that these physical features determine so much of any individual's social destiny that they must therefore be central to identity. So heavily do we rely on this combination of authorities that when we encounter persistent self-identification at odds with them—a self-identification that conflicts with the marks of physical descent—we often dismiss it as somehow false (one can't pretend to have a differently shaped and hued body than one has, can one?) and somehow wrong (isn't it immoral, or at least unattractively self-centered, to diminish solidarity with those with whom one shares a social destiny, however much that destiny may be the product of prejudicial treatment at the hands of empowered racists?).

We resist especially the substitution of civic-national ("I'm an American") and religious ("I'm a Christian") identities for descent community identities, apparently because such substitutions seem to be evasions of primal truths about "the way things are" and thus serve to invite the further victimization of peoples whose "true" interests are served by solidarity with their community of descent. We seem the most willing to accept multiple identities when there is a clear hierarchy placing identity by descent community first (ahead of identities by religion, civic nationality, sexual orientation, professional calling, and so on). And we seem the most willing to accept individual choice when it validates social expectations created by the physical marks of descent. In all these decisions we seem to regard identity as an essentially cultural phenomenon that exists within space largely determined by physical phenomena. Even when identity is conceived as a consciousness or subjectivity (as in "the Chicano subject" or "the white subject"), the ordinance of perceived shared physical descent over proclaimed individual consent is strong.

This authority of the physical marks of descent in the political economy of identity invites scrutiny in the context of liberal theory's commitment to expanding the perimeter of the freedom of individuals. We might suppose that liberal theory would favor identity choice over identity ascription, even though liberals sometimes do find that other considerations override individual choice. Consider four public policy issues that pit individual choice against an ostensibly justified constraint. All four issues are widely discussed by American liberals in our time.

One issue is the "right to work" rather than to be subjected to collective bargaining. Liberals usually say that the social benefits of collective bargaining easily trump the individual's choice of terms of employment. It's the conservatives who rejoice in the decline of unions. A second is flagged by the mantra "taxation is theft." Individuals ought to be able to choose how to spend what they earn, rather than have a certain percentage of their earnings taken by the state and then spent for them as the state sees fit. People on the left generally respond that a person's earnings are facilitated by governmental policies created by the national community as a whole, and insist that the interests of the society trump the individual's choice of how the entirety of his or her earnings should be expended. It's the far right that finds taxes problematic on principle. A third is what is increasingly called "school choice." Self-styled progressives usually defend the existing system of public schools as superior to a voucher system on the basis of the larger interest of the society. Equality in this view is more likely to be achieved by perfecting a system of public education universal to the society than by parceling out education into a series of tax-supported but de-facto private schools. It's the conservatives, again, who most push for vouchers. The fourth issue is reproductive choice. A woman should have access to contraceptives and abortion, rather than be subject to societal restrictions on her decision to become pregnant or to stay pregnant. Now in this case, unlike in the first three, liberal theorists almost always deny that sweeping restrictions on the reproductive choices of adult women are justified by some larger social interest. It is the political right wing that finds "pro-choice" a sham overruled by the social benefits of restraining individual choice. Liberals who resist certain other claims to choice offered in the name of an individual's freedom often defend reproductive choice vigorously, and with well-theorized confidence.

Identity choice—or solidarity choice—might well be compared with reproductive choice. Voluntary identities are surely to be preferred to ascribed identities on classically liberal grounds. Encouraging individuals to make their own decisions about cultural identity, about whom to affiliate with, about how to distribute their own capabilities for solidarity, would seem to be a classically liberal program. Such a program is of course embodied in the principle of "affiliation by revocable consent." Yet the widespread willingness to tolerate and even to encourage identity and solidarity ascription implies the contrary. Those who acquiesce in, or promote, identity and solidarity ascription implicitly count this restriction on choice as more comparable to collective bargaining and taxation and public schools than to restrictions on reproductive choice.

Is there any basis for such a determination? Some might say yes, at least for nonwhites, because choice undermines the solidarities that nonwhite ethno-racial groups need in a white-dominated society that persistently treats individuals differently according to color. The strongest argument for ascription in matters of identity/solidarity relies on the judgment that individuals, no matter what their subjective desires, in the objective world are going to be treated by society according to their color codes. In this view, the ethno-racial pentagon, even though the product of prejudicial treatment, gets right the lines that truly matter, and fussing with those lines merely evades the conditions under which the struggle for equality must be engaged. A certain amount of ascription of nonwhites is thus justified in the larger interest of nonwhites. Affiliation by revocable consent, in this view, is indeed like refusing to pay taxes or insisting on one's "right to work."

This line of reasoning is more often implied than actually argued. It invites a number of vital questions, including how one assesses and explains what progress the United States has managed to make in diminishing white racism. What this line of reasoning most requires, however, is an analysis of just how the forcing of people into identities they do not want can facilitate the liberation of those with the same ascribed identity.

Konrad Latte, a Holocaust survivor, shocked Israeli journalists when he told them that he did not consider himself to be a Jew. His only felt connection to Jewishness was having been persecuted as a Jew. He did not want to grant Hitler the authority to determine his identity, to tell him with whom to associate, even in the wake of the Shoah.[9] How should one respond when African Americans or Japanese Americans reject the authority of white racists to tell them who they are? When the Louisiana-born writer Anatole Broyard tried to enact such a rejection, he could get away with it, as Henry Louis Gates, Jr., has pointed out, only because Broyard was sufficiently light-skinned to pass as white throughout his career in New York City. Broyard did this at the cost of cutting off nearly all contact with his early life and his family of birth, and of being obliged to live his life under the principle of whiteness, which appears to have stunted his creativity as much as liberated it.[10]

Broyard's case raises the two connected issues of what it means to be white and what it means to exit from blackness or from any nonwhite group that has been stigmatized in the United States. If "whiting" is understood to mean only a passage into the freedom from stigma enjoyed by whites, and if "white" thus stands only for a social space within which individuals are not treated differently on account of their physical characteristics, there is no problem with a program that would "make everyone white." But if whiteness is instead taken to have a cultural content requiring those who pass into it to repudiate certain cultural choices, it becomes highly problematic—all the more so if the cultural content of whiteness is understood to include a propensity to stigmatize people who are dark. Then, any invitation to whiting risks retaining for the darkest of individuals the stigma from which lighter-skinned individuals—many persons of East Asian and Latin American origin, and of course "light-skinned blacks"—are being presumptively liberated.

Concern that the latter will result from the whiting of the not-really-really-black is of course fueled by awareness of the historical reality that Irish Americans, Jewish Americans, Italian Americans, and a number of other groups became white by virtue of having been successfully defined as not black. Yet the atmosphere at the turn of the twenty-first century is significantly different from that of earlier generations when these episodes of whiting took place. Then, black-white mixing was vehemently and often violently opposed on a large scale. Today, the very invidiousness of blackness is challenged by the proliferation of memoirs and treatises on mixed ancestries, and by the increased range and intensity of attacks on the one-drop rule that defined Broyard's choices. That invidiousness was expressed by the determination of empowered whites to segregate it entirely, even by treating as tainted anyone with so little "black blood" as Broyard. It is not unreasonable to hope that the more mixture is accepted, the less fear there will be of what is being mixed.[11]

Diminishing invidiousness will also, presumably, make strong affiliations with historically stigmatized descent communities more comfortable. The principle of revocable consent, as I explained in a sentence I took to be so important that I used it twice (13, 118), "supports the renewal and critical revision of those communities of descent whose progeny choose to devote their energies to these communities even after experiencing opportunities for affiliating with other kinds of people." This formulation was designed not only to acknowledge the value for many people of affiliation by descent communities but also to take into account a fact mentioned repeatedly in this book: that these "opportunities" now increase with whiteness and are too often limited by color prejudice on the part of empowered white people. From my coining of the phrase "Haley's Choice" onward throughout this book, I have identified traditional racism as the chief barrier to voluntary affiliation. A color hierarchy is the main force behind the practice of ascribing identities regardless of an individual's will and actual cultural orientation. Yet my assumption throughout has been that some people will have good reasons for choosing to identify with and contribute to their communities of descent even when prejudice does not eliminate the possibility of exit. The popularity of Jewish communal identity after the decline of ascription, and of anti-Jewish prejudice, is an example. After "liberation" some Jews lose interest in most things Jewish, but others renew Jewish ties. As a prominent scholar of American Jewish history has put the point, affiliated Jews in recent American history "would continue being Jews because they wanted to, not because they were being forced to."[12] Surely, this is as it should be.

Yet I encounter, again and again, the feeling that a true community, a true identity, must entail a significant element of coercion. True belonging, it is said, is not something to which you can consent. An affiliation consented to, in this view, is somehow less worthy and less real than an affiliation over which one has no control. To encounter this outlook is rather like talking with someone who does not believe in divorce. Is marriage a meaningful commitment only if there is never any possibility whatsoever of exit from it?

It is conceivable that within the next generation, Americans will find a way to decouple identity and solidarity. Perhaps they will develop a meaning for identity that will reserve to it some of the nonperformative elements of being and belonging that claim each of us, whatever our individual wishes may be. If so, perhaps they will simultaneously reserve to solidarity the complex of expectations and commitments that invite application of the principle of affiliation by revocable consent. But for now, Americans are still living in the era of identity/solidarity.

Yet these Americans possess, in their tradition of civic nationalism, more to offer to themselves and to the world than some of them realize. This brings me to the third point of tension between *Postethnic America* and some of its readers: the sense that the national project of the United States is too heavily encumbered by racism and imperialism to sustain even the modest democratic-egalitarian aspirations for it that I express.

The United States has so often failed its own citizens and abused the citizens of other nations that any effort to consolidate an American national "we" raises understandable suspicions. I urged that we look upon the national community of the United States as one solidarity among many, deeply flawed yet having some real virtues in a society increasingly stratified by class and in a world bedeviled by ethnic cleansing and the resurgence of blood-and-soil nationalism. I observed that the ideological resources and sheer power of the United States remain valuable to egalitarians and democrats. Amid multiple affiliations, including subnational and transnational political formations, there is good cause, I argued, to struggle for control over the American nation-state rather than to let it fall yet more fully into the hands of an internationally oriented business elite and the religious right.

Some readers, however, found me too hopeful about the potential of the national community to mitigate inequality at home, and others worried that my emphasis on the relatively nonethnic nationality of the United States was too conducive to the support of American political hegemony in the world. Instead of encouraging any kind of nationalism, should not American liberals be supporting transnational causes and the interests of diasporic minorities within the United States? Given the ease with which the affirmation of the national "we" has historically gotten out of control, fostering a conformist, 100-percent-Americanism, perhaps the national community has more than enough momentum already? And given the extraordinary global position now enjoyed by the United States, perhaps the last thing we need is another invitation to think positively about this country and its potential influence in the world?

These questions reflect the severe political disagreements that today swirl around the national project of the United States, especially within academia. In the spirit of these disagreements, some reviewers thought *Postethnic America* rather too patriotic, and others thought it distressingly the opposite. A sociologist, annoyed that I had not attacked the far right more aggressively, described me as a "neoconservative." Yet a bona fide conservative historian who writes for the *National Review* could identify a left-wing Berkeley liberal when he saw one. This reviewer doubted that "Americans would have held fast at Seminary Ridge or stormed the beaches of Normandy and Iwo Jima" for "cosmopolitan and multiculturalist" ideas like mine. He added that the "long-term threat to American nationality comes more from

Berkeley and Ann Arbor" than from the immigrant hordes of Los
Angeles and Miami to which his conservative comrades tend to
overreact.[13] I have little expectation of satisfying my critics on the
far right, but here I try to persuade other skeptical readers that
risking a good bit of political capital in the distinctive solidarity
of the United States is not a bad idea, given the available alternatives and the direction of the world.

A stronger national solidarity enhances the possibility of social and economic justice within the United States. This is a simple point, but an extremely important one. Any society that
cannot see its diverse members as somehow "in it together" is going to have trouble distributing its resources with even a modicum of equity. The United States has the lowest taxation rate in
the industrialized world, yet it is awash in efforts to reduce further the obligations that wealthy and even comfortably middle-
class Americans have for the basic health and well-being of the
rest of the population. The halting efforts in the direction of social democracy taken by the United States during the Progressive
Era, the New Deal, and the Great Society were predicated on a
strong national "we," as were the triumphs of the Civil Rights
movement. In more recent years, a relatively weak sense of national community has surely been a major factor in preventing
the United States from developing a system of national health
care comparable to those of most industrialized nations. This
weak sense of mutual obligation also facilitates the decay of the
public school system and its replacement by a series of radically
unequal private and public systems designed to serve the interests
of Americans of very different stations. Internet billionaires pro-

liferate, while many public services are inadequate and the prison population grows.

The attacks on the liberal state long fashionable among academic leftists have dovetailed with the antistatism of the Republicans to erode a political tradition that still has much to recommend it. Taking account of this, Bruce Robbins has sensibly speculated that "the only responsible politics for a more-than-academic left" would include "overcoming the militant antistatism of American voters and trying to give the United States something like the developed social welfare system characteristic of other highly industrialized nations."[14] The ideal of national solidarity as I defend it in *Postethnic America* is best understood, then, as directed more against "the separatism of the rich" than against the separatism of diasporic ethno-racial communities.[15]

The ethno-racial groups whose expressions of cultural particularity are sometimes said to portend the "balkanization of America" actually serve, in today's multiculturalist milieu, to diminish the danger that American nationalism will again take on the Anglo-Protestant tribalism that has often deformed it in the past, especially in the 1920s.[16] Numerous checks are now in place to keep the American ideal of nationality civic rather than ethnic. Nationalism is not of a piece, and the variety represented by the contemporary United States has much less blood-and-soil exclusivity than do many of the nationalist movements of today that sustain understandable suspicion of nationalism. I refer to the nationalist movements recently launched or renewed by Basques, Croats, Flemings, Kurds, Macedonians, Serbs, Sikhs, Slovaks, Tamils, and Ukrainians. The nationalism of the United States is less particularistic even than that of the Catalonians, Quebecois, or Scots.

The nationalist impulse of the present American moment differs, also, from that found in this country during the Progressive Era and the 1920s. The right-wing politicians and white-supremacist militias who today replay and extend the Anglo-Protestant chauvinism of Madison Grant are not to be ignored, but they are at the margins of American politics, as their predecessors decidedly were not. Anyone who thinks that the United States of the early twenty-first century is about to replay the nativist politics of the 1920s might imagine the conservative Republican candidate of 1924, Calvin Coolidge, trying to win votes by speaking Yiddish or Italian. Coolidge's counterpart of 2000, George W. Bush, was always glad for an opportunity to show off his Spanish. In 2000 even Bob Jones University, in South Carolina, abandoned its long-anomalous ban on black-white dating, while in 1924 it was still within the bounds of respectable public discussion among white conservatives to advocate exporting the entire black population to New Guinea and the Belgian Congo. The potential value of the national "we" for the citizens and noncitizen inhabitants of the United States is too great to be downplayed for fear that it will be taken over by proto-fascists. Such forces will loom all the larger in national politics if more space is left open for the flag-flying far right because the rest of us hide the Stars and Stripes in embarrassment and devote all our political energy to affiliations of more certain virtue but less certain strength.

The internal dynamics of American society are thus the primary context in which the national project of the United States deserves support. Another context, however, is the international space in which this project exemplifies and advances the ideal of a certain kind of solidarity.

The human needs for belonging and for collective action are pervasive and deep. They will be met, not always by democratic nation-states open to persons of a variety of descent communities. Solidarities will form; the question is how people allocate their political energies between the various solidarities that are within their reach. And their reach, of course, will be limited by circumstances. Within the reach of citizens of the United States is a solidarity that, by virtue of the varieties of humankind it manages to embrace under a civic principle of nationality, may help the species diminish its traditional fear of intimacy across ethno-racial lines.

One striking feature of the national solidarity of the United States that enables it to play a small but significant role in the diminution of invidious marks of descent is the relative looseness of boundaries between many groups. The rate of marriage and reproduction across ethno-racial lines has been increasing rapidly even during decades when assimilation has been severely criticized in the name of the preservation of the integrity of descent communities. Census data from 1990 revealed that 81 percent of married Polish Americans between the ages of twenty-five and thirty-four had married outside their ethnic group, and that 73 percent of Italian Americans had done so. Data from 1990 is already a decade out of date, but it contains evidence of rapid structural assimilation even of non-European descent communities. The statistics about non-European groups demand emphasis, given the long-term history of Eurocentric attitudes in the United States. After all, we are talking about a nation that did not even allow Asian immigrants to become naturalized citizens until 1952. Of married persons between the ages of twenty-five and thirty-four in 1990 who had been born in the United States, about one-half of those with Asian ancestry had outmarried. Among Hispanics, about 35 percent had acquired a spouse of non-Latino descent. About 60 percent of Indians reported being married to non-Indians. Black-white marriages continued to be rare, but they were considerably more frequent than they had been only a few decades previously. In 1990, 3.75 percent of married black women between twenty-five and thirty-four years of age were married to white men, and 8.5 percent of the married black men were wedded to white women.[17]

These last figures concerning black-white unions provide little support for the predictions of some social commentators that ethno-racial distinctions will disappear in the twenty-first century. Blacks still marry outside their descent community at a much lower rate than do other nonwhites. But these statistics do indicate an extent of black-white mixing significant for a society that in 1990 stood only twenty-three years from *Loving v. Virginia*, when the United States Supreme Court ruled unconstitutional all state laws forbidding interracial marriage. Until that ruling of 1967, black-white marriages were illegal in many of the states in which a large percentage of the population was black. An intriguing feature of the increase in black-white marriages is their location in very different parts of the class structure: enlisted personnel in the military and doctoral graduates of elite universities are among those most likely to marry across the black-white color line.

When all these results of the 1990 census are considered in relation to the rest of the world, the old notion of the United States as a melting pot regains some of its credibility, although devoid, of course, of the sense of natural progression so long innocently associated with quotations from Crèvecoeur and Zangwill. A political and legal struggle that continues today has been required to diminish the ethnocentric social attitudes and public policies put in place and long enforced by dominant Anglo-Protestants. But the United States now displays a degree of structural assimilation not to be found even in such other diverse societies as India, Switzerland, and Belgium, to say nothing of more homogeneous societies like Germany, Japan, the Netherlands, Austria, and Poland. The Belgian case is worth special mention because there the "diversity" consists largely of two groups of white European Catholics who, from the point of view of the average Californian, might appear to be Tweedledum and Tweedledee. But the Flemings and the Walloons pursue a language-based identity politics ferocious enough to threaten the existence of their shared nation-state and to make virtually impossible the assimilation into either Dutch- or French-speaking Belgium of people who are yet more different: the darker-skinned Muslims who have immigrated from Turkey and Morocco.

The most distinctive aspect of American "diversity" is thus not simply the great variety of descent communities visible in the United States. Rather, it also consists in the millions of people who share openly in two or more of the standardized descent communities. But there is yet more to it. What is of greater world-historical significance is the frequency with which the descent communities that are considered standard change from generation to generation. The historical process by which a number of European-based immigrant groups became "white" has been widely discussed by historians. The whiting of economically successful Asian Americans is a staple of everyday conversation in California, where Japanese Americans were taken off to concentration camps only two generations before. Yet the most historically salient case is that of American Jews. As recently as 1940 Jews were a stigmatized group often called a race, only about 3 percent of whom had outmarried. They were systematically excluded, by legal authority, from many spheres of employment, housing, and public accommodations. Yet by the 1980s between one-third and one-half of all marriages involving Jews entailed the acquiring of a non-Jewish spouse, and Jews had become so thoroughly assimilated into the "European" community of descent that they had ceased to be counted as a distinctive descent community when issues of ethno-racial representation and underrepresentation were discussed.

Many other nations are also diverse by virtue of having more than one prominent descent community. But in many of those countries—Indonesia, Belgium, India, Kenya, Switzerland, and Nigeria are convenient examples—diversity is manifest in several historically continuous descent communities that remain sharply separate from one another. One need not fall into the trap of a mystical "American exceptionalism" to recognize empirically warranted differences between the United States and certain other specific nations and to appreciate the value of any political order that diminishes the constraints that often follow from ascribed status according to descent. The United States may not be unique, but it is a formidable engine of ethno-racial change. In this modest respect, the United States since 1945, for all its manifestly counterrevolutionary actions in Vietnam and Guatemala, in Chile and the Congo, has proved to be a revolutionary power.

This is not to imply that Americans thinking about marrying and having children should regard it as a patriotic duty to find a mate from a different ethno-racial bloc. Freedom from imperatives of this kind, not the embrace of them, is the point. It is in support of greater freedom of family-making choice, not of greater constraints on such choice, that the recent demographic history of the United States bears witness among its own citizens and to the world.

Yet the very idea that the United States might serve as a valuable example to the world of a certain kind of civic nation mediating between the species and multiple communities of descent needs to be carefully formulated. I refer to an example, not a model. The historical particularity of each nation's situation militates against so arrogant a notion as a model to be copied, especially when the candidate for model status is the world's preeminent military and economic power. I use the word *example* in what might be called its softest sense: it is simply a case that can be scrutinized critically by people who have reason to be interested in it. And now, when so many countries, especially in Europe, contemplate a future with larger immigrant populations, there is global interest in political communities that cross ethno-racial barriers without pretending to be universal.

Postethnic America is a frankly Americocentric book. I am more concerned to clarify and comment critically on the national project of the United States than I am to offer more than the most general of ideas about how other national projects, with different constitutional traditions and different social structures, might deal with communities of descent. My defense of liberal nationalism is highly context-specific and falls well short of a universal theory of the sort developed recently by a number of political scientists and philosophers.[18] One of the latter, however, has voiced a concern that I want to address here. The Canadian philosopher Will Kymlicka worries that the American example, particularly when understood in the terms I advance in this book, is having a pernicious influence in countries that have "national minorities" rather than simply "immigrant groups."[19]

Kymlicka distinguishes sharply between these two types of groups. What he calls a "national minority" is a people "involuntarily incorporated into a larger state, as a result of colonization, conquest, or the ceding of territory from one imperial power to another." His examples within western democracies include the Catalans and the Basques in Spain, the Scots and the Welch in the United Kingdom, and the Quebecois and indigenous peoples in Canada. These national minorities, and others found in Central and Eastern Europe, often "seek control over the language and curriculum of schooling in their region" and sometimes not only adopt an ideology of nationhood but demand some form of political autonomy short of secession, which is also a goal for some. Kymlicka complains that nation-states trying to work out fair accommodations with these national minorities are not helped by

American slogans such as "individual rights, not group rights." Indeed, the ideology of civic as opposed to ethnic nationality has become a tool in the hands of majority nationalists who "crush minority nationalism" and "strip national minorities of their separate public institutions and rights of self-government." Kymlicka cites examples of the latter in Slovakia, Romania, Serbia, and Russia. When it comes to countries dealing with immigrant groups, however, he generously endorses "Hollinger's account of a postethnic America" as "a good model," from which "countries like Austria and Belgium could learn a great deal."[20]

I agree that the nation-states of Central and Eastern Europe, and many of those in other parts of the world that fall outside the scope of Kymlicka's North Atlantic focus, require a politics more complicated than a banning of group rights in the interests of an American-style individualism. Yet on basic human rights grounds I worry more than Kymlicka does about the repression that can take place within the national minorities of which he is so protective. Territories dominated by Kymlicka's "national minorities" often include other minorities, as is true in much of Balkan Europe. I do not doubt that limited autonomy for territorially concentrated and culturally homogeneous minority groups in some nation-states will prove to be a better solution than forced assimilation or secession, but the less territorially concentrated and the less culturally homogeneous the group, the less justification for dismissing the experience of the United States as an irrelevant distraction. And in the great calculus of atrocities, the depredations committed in the name of civic nationality should not be considered in isolation from those committed in the name of ethnic integrity. The civic-inspired violence to which Kymlicka refers may have less to do with the ideal of civic nationality than with the lack of democratic political culture. I agree that the particular circumstances of each country will put practical limits on whatever balance emerges between civic and ethnic principles for political community. But I am less willing than Kymlicka appears to be to relax the tension between the claims of the tribe and the claims of the human, and to carve out political space in which the tribe simply rules. And I am less confident that the national minorities in democratic and nondemocratic states fall into a class sufficiently unified to be theorized about in the same terms.

It is only when addressing cases within democratic states of the North Atlantic west that Kymlicka develops his most pointed argument for group rights for national minorities. He declares that the minority nationalisms of Quebec, Scotland, and Catalonia are all "postethnic in Hollinger's sense." He concedes that Basque and Flemish nationalisms, by contrast, are more racial in orientation. Kymlicka's evidence that Quebec displays "just the sort of fluid hybridic multiculturalism . . . that Hollinger endorses" is worth quoting because it displays a turn in his argument on which I want to comment:[21]

> Quebec accepts immigrants from all over the world: it has roughly the same per capita rate of immigration as the United States. . . . The province administers its own immigration program, actively recruiting immigrants, most of whom are nonwhite. These immigrants are not only granted citizenship under relatively easy terms, but are encouraged

by Quebec's own "interculturalism" policy to interact with the members of other ethnic groups, to share their cultural heritage, and to participate in common public institutions. . . . Far from trying to preserve some sort of racial purity, Quebec nationalists are actively seeking people of other races, cultures, and faiths to join them, integrate with them, intermarry with them, and jointly help build a modern, pluralist, distinct (French-speaking) society in Quebec.

What I find remarkable about this account is its implication that Quebec is potentially a civic nation virtually identical to the United States, except that the official language is French instead of English. What, other than linguistic particularism, makes Quebec by Kymlicka's description any more a national minority in Canada than New Jersey or Colorado is a national minority in the United States? Kymlicka is right to complain that I grouped Quebec unfairly with a number of other nationalist movements that are more ethno-racially exclusive. But the more we are asked to see Quebec as a proto-nation of immigrants, the less claim Quebec has, by Kymlicka's own standards, to standing as a national minority, and the less salience his key example has to the general argument he seeks to advance.[22]

The power of Kymlicka's pivotal distinction between national minorities and immigrant groups is further weakened by his proper admission that the distinction is of no help in understanding the situation of blacks in the United States. Nor, one might add, does this distinction precisely take account of the historical situation of Mexican Americans, overwhelmingly immigrant on Kymlicka's terms but living to a significant extent on land taken from Mexico by conquest in 1848.[23] Even in Europe, the distinction appears not to do as much analytic work as Kymlicka asks it to. Do the Tyrol Germans really have a better claim to group rights in Italy than do Turkish immigrants in Belgium or mixed-descent East Indians in the Netherlands? Are claims for group rights that might be advanced on behalf of the Muslim "guest workers" of some Western European nations, marginalized as they often are from the full benefits of citizenship, so much weaker than those advanced on behalf of the Scots in the United Kingdom, who have obtained considerable benefit from three centuries of union with England?

The point of the "example" of the United States, then, is not to serve as a panacea for the problems of diversity abroad. If the United States can help the species find a future in which the varieties of humankind are less afraid of intimacy with one another, and can draw its various circles of "we" more deliberately and less prejudicially, that will be all to the good. Scrutiny of the United States is often cut off prematurely by the valid but imperfectly contextualized complaint that the black-white color line continues to mock American ideals of ethno-racial equality, and that European and Asian ethnic groups have gotten ahead in American society partly by defining themselves as not black. The missing context is that many countries of the world experience ferocious antagonism, prejudice, and discrimination *within* populations that are entirely white or entirely black. This is so, for example, in Northern Ireland and in Israel. The same is true in Rwanda, Nigeria, and Kenya. Hence the mixing of white descent communities in the

United States is of more than trivial significance. To say this need not be an invitation for banal and distracting debates over whether the moral glass of the nation is half-empty or half-full, and whether antiblack racism is anomalous or structural to the public culture of the United States.

The degree of mixing found in the United States is all the more important because the United States is evidently and deeply marked by racism. If it were not, the ethno-racial mixing found there would be of less interest to other societies that must grapple with racism. The case of the United States, depending on the specific path it follows, may yet serve humbly to remind a heavily racialized world that even a society with a deeply racist past can incorporate individuals from a great variety of communities of descent on terms of considerable intimacy within a civic solidarity.

Reference to civic solidarity calls forth the matter with which I want to conclude this postscript. During my discussion of the three major points of tension between *Postethnic America* and potentially sympathetic readers, and throughout this book, I have alluded repeatedly to the United States as a civic nation. This use of the classical distinction between civic and ethnic is sound, but the distinction can be drawn too sharply. With the case of the United States in view, I want to elaborate here on my observation that this distinction "eventually breaks down because over the course of time civic affiliations can help to create those that are eventually recognized as ethnic" (160).

Ethnic communities are historically contingent entities. The community of descent of modern England is a convenient example. Even when the Scots and the Welsh are excluded, the population of England itself is the product of centuries of mixing of what were once distinctive communities of descent. As mixture of descent increases in the United States, the integrity of the old, standardized communities of descent is weakened. The greater the number of Americans who claim more than one descent community, the less ordinance does any one of these communities have over the others, and the more room is made in an individual's inventory of identities for the national community as a descent community of a kind: a kind produced not only by the mixing of genes but also by the shared memories and practices that are said to be essential to any sustaining solidarity.

The shared memories and practices are more than the set of procedures and rules that make up the constitutional order of the United States. The nation is a finite historical entity with a record of specific tragedies, successes, failures, contradictions, and provincial conceits sometimes missed by theorists eager to treat it as a set of abstractions. Theorists skeptical of the notion of a national culture sometimes underestimate the extent to which the United States can become, for some of its citizens, a solidarity to which one is attached with the same sense of belonging conventionally associated with ethnic communities.[24] Not every person develops the same kinds of feelings for it, and I am not saying that they should. But for the United States in 2000, an accurate historical narrative responsive to the nation's contemporary engagements and world-historical situation can do something to keep the national solidarity tight enough to mobilize action on common challenges and loose enough to militate against a replay of the chauvinisms of the past.

What such a narrative can do is to tell forthrightly the story of how the boundaries of the nation came into being, how and when they were challenged and sometimes changed, and by whom, and at what cost. How has the United States drawn and redrawn its social borders to accommodate, repel, or subjugate this or that group? How has racism and the struggle against it proceeded in a sequence of distinctive settings? Answers to these questions are among the proudest products of recent scholarship.[25] The answers can be part of the story the nation tells to itself and to the world. This story can be told without precluding the telling of other empirically warranted stories about subnational and transnational solidarities, including communities of descent.

The United States now finds itself in a position to develop and act upon a cultural self-image as *a national solidarity committed—but often failing—to incorporate individuals from a great variety of communities of descent, on equal but not homogeneous terms, into a society with democratic aspirations inherited largely from England*. There is much more to the United States than this. But if one were obliged to sum up in one sentence what a history of the United States is a history *of,* this sentence has much to recommend it beyond its simple truthfulness. It emphasizes the liberal and cosmopolitan elements of the national self-image without denying the parts of American history that are not liberal and not cosmopolitan.

This modest charter for national narrative expresses the vital idea that people can be politically equal without being culturally identical, yet it does not insist that history has enacted this ideal. It acknowledges the individualistic focus of the American polity; individuals, not groups, are incorporated into the nation. This conception of the national story enables the historian to display two truths often resisted by much of the public: the great extent to which the flourishing of the United States has depended on the exploitation of nonwhites, and the relative weakness, during most of the national history, of egalitarian ideals. This one-sentence charter for a narrative of the United States also acknowledges that the democratic aspirations of the Republic derived primarily—although not exclusively—from England, the European country from which virtually all political leaders of the Revolutionary generation directly descended. To recognize the heavily English foundation for the Constitution of the United States is not to preclude the study of other influences, nor to imply that people today of English descent have any greater personal connection to the constitutional order of the United States than does anyone else. But the reference to England does remind us of the particularity of history.

And it is the historical particularity of the United States that gives it something of the flavor of a community of descent. The United States is not a young country. No other major nation in the twenty-first century operates on the basis of a constitution written in the eighteenth. The two-and-a-quarter centuries of this nation's history, moreover, have been claimed as their own by individual members of an imposing succession of descent communities while experiencing varying degrees of assimilation, mistreatment, and worldly success. Whatever else the United States may be, it is a historically particular entity that often has been, and can be even more effectively in the future, an instrument for worthy transnational ends. Among the most worthy of these is the project of liberating human selves from the color-coded prisons in which they have been locked by "time's blood-rusted key."

Berkeley, California

June 2000

Ethnoracial Mixing
and Economic Segregation

The basic perspective sketched in *Postethnic America* is more widely accepted in 2005 than it was in 2000, when I last updated this book. Yet as the overlapping debates about cultural diversity, ethnoracial categories, identity, inequality, and American nationality move farther in the directions I hoped they would, certain issues become sharpened and more demanding of sustained attention. In this "Postscript 2005" I want to flag some of the ways in which this book has become more mainstream while standing still, and I want to identify and pursue briefly several of the specific issues that recent shifts in popular and scholarly opinion have placed at the center of the discussion. In so doing I will develop further the ideas that animate this book and try to show their increasing pertinence to current and ongoing challenges.[1]

Nothing makes *Postethnic America* more mainstream in 2005 than its key normative principle of "affiliation by revocable consent," holding that individuals ought to be encouraged to decide just how much of their own energies are to be devoted to their communities of descent. The practice of confidently telling people what their identity is or isn't has gone into precipitous decline as more and more Americans recognize that identity is performative. Identity is a code word for solidarity: to prescribe an identity for someone is to tell that person with whom they should be affiliating. The multiculturalism of the 1990s carried the deeply anti-individualist, anti-voluntarist expectation that individuals would naturally accept the cultural, social, and political habits popularly ascribed to their communities of descent, rather than form their own associations to the extent that their life-circumstances permitted choices. Important theoretical treatises by Kwame Anthony Appiah, Seyla Benhabib, Rogers Brubaker, Amy Gutmann, John Lie, Rogers Smith, and others have defended descent-defined solidarities, not as natural consequences of human difference but in their capacity as chosen instruments for political action and social support.[2]

Such affiliations, designed to advance some common purpose, can be vital means of seeking political justice and providing individuals with a life-sustaining sense of belonging, but they need not be permanent, need not be exclusive of other affiliations, and need not carry the pernicious assumption that color and culture go together. This last assumption, against which so much of *Postethnic America* is explicitly directed, is now under attack in countless books, essays, and op-ed columns. Richard Ford's *Racial Culture: A Critique* is a convenient example.[3] The rapid growth of a new cosmopolitan movement in this country and abroad is another example of how *Postethnic America* is now much less counter to the winds of doctrine than when it first appeared.[4] So is the flowering of a robust civic nationalism that argues for the importance of a strong American state even while subjecting to slashing critique the specific policies of the U.S. government since September 11, 2001.[5]

Welcome as these changes are to me, I can claim little credit for them. I am but one of many voices to have complained, from the mid-1990s onward, about the constraints of orthodox multiculturalism that are now so widely recognized. But one now widely used concept for which I can claim credit is "the ethnoracial pentagon." I coined this term in a paper of 1992 that first explored the main ideas I later developed in *Postethnic America*.[6] Looking for a word to denote the color coded, five-part demographic structure in which Americans had come to routinely classify themselves and each other (black, brown, red, white, and yellow) and contemplating the striking difference between it and the "Triple Melting Pot" that had been a popular figure of speech in the 1950s and 1960s (referring to Protestants, Catholics, and Jews), I hit upon this figure of speech. There must have been a real need for it, as it stuck and has now become part of the standard vocabulary of social scientists and historians, even many who are less concerned than I am about the constraining effects of this system of classification.[7]

The same cannot be said for *postethnic*. The term, which I first picked up from Werner Sollors (see page 243, n.5), now appears with some frequency even in the titles of books and essays that owe nothing to my influence.[8] But the ideas I tried to connect with this word have proved considerably more popular than the label I affixed to them. Contrary to my expectations in 1995, the word *cosmopolitanism* has come to denote a family of outlooks that can be distinguished from those I call "pluralist" and "universalist" (see pages 84–86). Most of the utterances that now get called "cosmopolitan" celebrate cultural diversity, as carried by different communities of descent; promote multiple and dynamic solidarities of varying scope; and recognize the need for sustaining intimate communities as well as the need for instruments capable of dealing with species-wide challenges. These preoccupations are especially evident in the popularity of such labels as "rooted cosmopolitanism," "cosmopolitan patriotism," and "critical cosmopolitanism," all designed to display a down-to-earth sensibility often said to be fatally absent in the classical cosmopolitanism associated with Kant and other eighteenth-century thinkers. The word *postethnic* may continue to help focus thinking in these cosmopolitan directions, and I shall continue to use it toward that end, while recognizing that the word's greatest currency has proven to be in relation to one specific kind of cosmopolitanism: the critical assessment of the claims on an individual made by, or on behalf of, a descent community. Hence the "post-black" discourse parallels almost exactly what I have been arguing about ethnoracial identities/affiliations generally: it is not that blackness is erased, but the extent and character of its ordinance over an individual's politics, values, art, or lifestyle is not taken for granted.[9]

But much remains contested, and just what lies "beyond multiculturalism" is being vigorously debated. We can best understand and engage these debates if we approach them in the context of two major trends in American society that have brought them to their present focus. One trend is demographic mixture. Self-identifying Hispanics, Asian Americans, and American Indians continue to select spouses outside their descent communities, and even the rate of black-white marriages is increasing.[10] The other trend is economic stratification. The gap between rich and poor is widening, and the number of poor and almost-poor is increasing at a rapid rate.[11] While more and more people are creating families across ethnoracial lines and many more additional people now find such mixing socially acceptable, fewer and fewer families of any ancestry or of any opinions can buy homes and educate children without two incomes. Patterns of income distribution in our own era are strikingly different from the three decades immediately following World War II. The economy has grown by 75 percent per capita since the 1970s, but the average wage for male workers has remained the same. The income ladder is now so much longer and rungs on the ladder are so much farther apart than they used to be that a worker rising at the same velocity as he or she did in the 1950s or 1960s would still be way behind the well-to-do. These trends were visible when *Postethnic America* was first published in 1995 and were even more pronounced when I updated the book in 2000. Yet as these trends continue to intensify early in our new century,[12] they invite amplification of the perspective sketched in this book.

Mixture is far from blotting out the role of ethnoracial differences in creating inequalities in American life.[13] The physical marks of descent can still disadvantage individuals, but many of the most persistent and easily measured disadvantages suffered by persons of non-European ancestry are now more difficult to sort out from the class position in which these Americans are so often locked. An emblem for this difficulty is the fact that the poorest of the residents of New Orleans, uniquely unprotected from Hurricane Katrina on August 29, 2005 and uniquely neglected in the notoriously ineffective rescue efforts that followed, were also the blackest. It will not do to deny that color helped to lock those Americans into the low class position that structured their fate in New Orleans. The overwhelming majority of residents without automobiles, and thus without an ability to evacuate, were black. Yet even the most dark-skinned of immigrants from the Caribbean, Africa, and South Asia often do better in general throughout the United States than do lighter-skinned "African Americans" whose opportunities to overcome the legacies of slavery and Jim Crow have been diminished by economic segregation. Hence *Postethnic America*'s argument that a multiculturalism organized around the classic color categories could provide little traction in the struggle for a more equal society now strikes me as more sound than ever, as does this book's insistence that mixture should be near the center of our analysis of the ethnoracial past, present, and future of the United States. The assumption of classical multiculturalism that the standardized, color-coded descent groups were durable, clearly bounded entities around which social policy, education, and political lobbying could be confidently organized becomes less defensible by the day.[14]

Amid the ruins of the old multiculturalism and in the verbal breezes generated by ethnoracial mixing and economic segregation, there arise a series of sharpened, demanding issues to which the perspective outlined in *Postethnic America* speaks. One has to do with the old concept of "race": should it simply be dropped or instead redefined in order to convey new meanings? A second issue concerns the differences in historical experience between several distinctive communities of descent often grouped together as "people of color." How significant are these differences? A third revolves around the system of classification employed by the U.S. Census. Does the government use the right categories, even when allowing individuals to identify with more than one ethnoracial group? I want to take up these three issues, one by one.

An imposing range of criteria are now invoked to assess the value of the concept of "race."[15] Almost everyone agrees that races do not exist in the sense so long assumed—biological entities carrying vastly different potentials for intelligence and social behavior, justifying the invidious treatment of inferior races—and almost everyone agrees, further, that the "racializing" of human beings, entailing their being treated differently on account of their perceived marks of descent, continues on a large scale. Yet some say that it is proper to denote as a "race" the people who have been racialized while others say it is not. To continue to speak of "races," complain the critics, perpetuates unintentionally too many of the old racist connotations. Better to speak of "racialized persons" or to diminish the invidiousness of *race* by speaking of *ethnoracial groups*, thus blurring the line between *race* and *ethnicity*. Defenders of the old vocabulary argue instead that it is right to speak of races because now we understand the meaning of *race* very differently, as a social rather than a biological reality. Some champions of the concept assert that if we abandon the concept of race we risk pretending that the inequalities created by the process of racialization are less severe than they truly are; others, suspicious of narratives of victimization that assign group-defining power to oppressors, place more emphasis on a given group's will to preserve itself as a group, on its own agency as a "race." The conversation among social constructionists is thus complicated by the fact that some of them want to retain the term for quite opposite reasons: one, to mark the power of racists to racialize and demean people of a given descent, and second, to mark the substantiality of a community and the integrity of its efforts to survive as a solidarity. In the meantime, resounding voices in the biomedical sciences insist that the concept of race still has genuine utility after it is separated rigorously from the mistakes and prejudices of old-fashioned racial science.[16] What the biomedical defenders of the concept of race have in mind is quite different, however, from the meaning of the term implied by social scientists and political activists, such as those lobbying for the idea that Latinos are a race rather than just an ethnic group.

My summary statement in the main text (page 39) that "racism is real but races are not" and my persistent use of *ethnoracial* puts me among those who suspect that *race* unmodified at this point in our history can do little but confuse us. Yet the geneticists make a strong case.[17] I believe it does make sense to carve out a clearly defined, technical discourse in which the word can be part of the evolving vocabulary for analyzing the differentiation of the human species. But the more distinctly biological the usage of *race* becomes, the less credible become the arguments for this word's other employments. No doubt some words can be popularly understood to mean slightly different things in different contexts when the boundaries between the contexts are clear and the use of words is consistent. But the history of *race* and the likelihood that it will continue to have some currency in science—an authority so often invoked by racists of the most destructive sort—makes it extremely unlikely that it can be one of those words carrying context-dependent meanings at odds with one another. The United States will be well served by dropping the word from the most portentous public space in which the currency of the word in its openly nonscientific meaning is perpetuated, the federal census, about which I have more to say below.[18] Social constructionists of different persuasions were already up against a real challenge in trying to replace an outmoded biocentric understanding of *race* with a new social one, but now the new appeal of a notion of race that is not socially constructed weakens yet more the project of saving, for nonbiological public use in highly politicized contexts, a word whose power derives overwhelmingly from its biological history.

The best discussion of the process of racialization and of the need for a vocabulary that can recognize its results is Lawrence Blum's book of 2002, *"I'm Not a Racist, But. . . ": The Moral Quandary of Race*.[19] Blum prefers the awkwardness of *racialized groups* to the commonsense simplicity of *race*: we are better off speaking in ways that acknowledge the complexities masked by the simple language of "common sense." Blum finds *ethnoracial groups* "felicitous," but he is correct to observe that this phrase does not carry senses of "stigma, discrimination, and hierarchy."[20] *Ethnoracial* is not a term of my invention, but its use to blur the distinction between "races" and "ethnic groups" was still unusual when literary theorist David Theo Goldberg and I and a few others employed it pointedly in the early 1990s.[21] By the summer of 2005 this ostensibly oxymoronic word had yet to find its way into the online *Merriam-Webster's Dictionary*, but the search engine Google could turn up 8,830 references to it in .04 seconds.[22] Surely, the rapid acceptance of this word where people used to say "race and ethnicity," or one or the other, is a mark of the more critical tone that has come to the discussion of descent groups in the United States and abroad. *Ethnorace* performs a vital service: it denotes all descent-defined population groups, recognizing that all have properties that sometimes have been called "ethnic" and "racial" (whites/Caucasians/Euro Americans, we should remember, have often been called a "race" and still are by the Census Bureau) and sets aside the task of distinguishing the groups that have done the racializing from those that have been racialized, and to what degree. But this other task turns out to be not so difficult, even when we proceed without the help of *race*.

These distinctions are indeed at the heart of the second of the newly sharpened issues I want to address here. How significant are the differences in American experience of the various, specific non-European-derived populations? *Postethnic America* is broadly "African American exceptionalist" in outlook because it treats the experience of black people in American society as unique, a theme I developed further in "Postscript 2000" (esp. 176–177). This special character of black experience now demands a yet more emphatic underscoring.

The question of difference versus similarity of experience from one minority group to another gains special importance from the widespread presumption, reflected in many government-sponsored and privately supported entitlement programs, that all descent groups not popularly regarded as white (which includes Hispanics, often officially classified as white but often treated as nonwhite) have been more or less equally victimized by white racism. The remarkable story of how American Indians, Asian Americans, and Hispanic Americans came to be regarded as "like blacks" is well told in recent books by John Skrentny and Hugh Davis Graham.[23] But the presumption has implications beyond affirmative action. It affects the basic terms on which Americans of different descent groups see themselves and each other.

The presumption that all "people of color"—the four nonwhite segments of the ethnoracial pentagon—have been abused more or less equally is often just that, an idea truly presumed, that is, taken so for granted that it requires no argumentation. But the idea has been explicitly defended in some very prominent venues. A conspicuous example is the 1998 report of President Clinton's Initiative on Race, *One America in the 21st Century: Forging a New Future.*[24] This report, the only president-commissioned inquiry into "race" since the Kerner Commission of thirty years before, systematically suppressed evidence that Americans of Asian descent, of Hispanic or American Indian origin, were any less fatally the victims of white racism than were African Americans. All but five of the Clinton Commission's more than fifty recommendations were general to all victims of white racism, and none of the exceptions speak to the specific claims of African Americans on the national conscience.[25]

Yet blacks, and blacks alone, inherit a multi-century legacy of group-specific enslavement, Jim Crow discrimination, and hypodescent racialization (invidious classification on the basis of "one drop of blood") long carried out under constitutional authority in the United States, to say nothing of extralegal, terror-enforced political intimidation. The Clinton Commission was understandably determined to refute the myth that "the problem of racial intolerance in this country has been solved," but in its reluctance to particularize and measure the dimensions of this problem and to deal directly with the reasons why some Americans mistakenly believe the problem to be solved, the commission ended up weakening its case. The more honestly that each group's destiny in the United States is analyzed in particular, and in comparison with the others, the more evident it becomes that economic position, commercially marketable skills, and education prior to immigration have a huge impact on the success with which immigrants and their descendants are able to overcome the worse consequences of the white racism they encounter. Chihuahuan agricultural laborers and Bengali engineers really do bring to the United States radically different pre-emigration resources that affect not only their own lives, but the lives of their children and grandchildren.[26]

The fact that Americans with origins in China, Korea, Japan, and Vietnam average a higher household income and greater educational attainments than even Americans of European ancestry is now well known and is increasingly understood to be a consequence of historical circumstances. As upward mobility into "the middle class" becomes more limited in general, the African American descendants of slaves and the least educated of recent immigrants—illegal and legal—from poor counties in Mexico are among the people most obviously segregated by economic stratification. To appreciate the differences between the experiences of the descendants of slaves and of the descendants of recent immigrants from China, Guatemala, Korea, Mexico, Japan, the Philippines, and other countries around the globe is not to deny that all of these people were subject to mistreatment. Our historians, social scientists, and journalists have documented this mistreatment in detail, including the genocide, the land-owning restrictions, the school segregation, and the prohibitions on naturalization and cross-group marriage that have affected many different groups of Americans at different times. The point is not to ignore a structure of inequality and disadvantage, but rather to assess that structure more precisely.

Economically measurable differences between the various minority descent communities is not the only reality to undercut the old presumption that the varieties of Hispanic Americans, Asian Americans, and American Indians were all "like blacks" in their historical circumstances. This presumption has been further undercut by another portentous recognition: demographic mix-ing has been a dramatically different experience for African Americans than for anyone else. Much of the mixture of white and black visible in the skin of many African Americans is the legacy of sexual exploitation of slave females by empowered white men. And no group was as deeply affected by miscegenation laws as were black Americans, the bulk of whom were subject to those laws until ruled unconstitutional in 1967. The practice of hypode-scent racialization, moreover, was never applied to any other group on remotely the same scale and with the same persistence as it has been applied to people with any discernable trace of what was once called "Negro" ancestry. The special form of white racism enacted through the principle of hypodescent was cast into bold relief in the 1980s and 1990s by the dramatic upsurge of im-migration from Latin America and Asia. The first of these immi-grations displayed from the start an acknowledged and often celebrated mixture of European and indigenous ancestry and pro-duced children who married Anglos at a rising rate and who were not subject to hypodescent racialization as Latinos. The new im-migrants from Asia married Anglos at a considerably higher rate than Latinos did, and their offspring were not socially coerced to identify as 100 percent Asian. In the meantime, the population of American Indians increased several times over, not as a result of biological reproduction but by masses of people newly declaring themselves to be of Indian ancestry, much less subject to stigma, of course, than black ancestry.[27]

The unprecedented amount of public attention paid in very recent years to the reality of black-white mixing and to its systematic erasure by the one-drop rule is a distinctive episode in American cultural and intellectual history. In *The Human Stain* and *The Time of Our Singing*, Philip Roth and Richard Powers, two of the nation's most morally serious and artistically skilled writers of fiction, produced major novels on these themes in 2000 and 2003.[28] DNA evidence lends new credibility to old, widely denounced claims that Thomas Jefferson fathered children with his slave, Sally Hemings. In 2003, one-time segregationist leader Senator Strom Thurmond was revealed to have fathered a daughter with a youthful black maid when he was a young man. Dozens of family memoirs, biographies, and autobiographies now tell stories of mixing and its denial. Tiger Woods, Mariah Carey, and other mixed-descent celebrities proclaim their blackness along with their whiteness and sometimes other color-coded aspects of their personal ancestry. Shelves full of popular and scholarly books explore, celebrate, and meditate upon mixtures of any and all colors, especially black and white.[29] Organizations devoted to support of mixed-ancestry Americans proliferate. Never since its legal and social consolidation in the 1920s has the one-drop rule been subject to such sustained, critical discussion.

Marriages across the black-white color line as conventionally understood (anyone who looks at all black is on the black side of the line) remain rare, but their number is increasing about seven times more rapidly than are other kinds of marriage. As registered by the Census Bureau, black-white marriages increased by about 70 percent between 1990 and 2000, while the total number of marriages in the United States during that decade increased by less than 9 percent.[30] Given the fact that marriage is less and less popular in the United States, another finding of the Census may be more significant: non-marital co-habitation across the black-color line in 2000 was about twice as common as black-white marriage.[31] With each passing year statistics of this kind prove more difficult to collect. As more Americans declare themselves to be in more than one color group, the color line loses the sharpness that enables measurement. Yet my point here turns more on the changed consciousness about the mixing that has already taken place than on the increased rate of black-white couplings. It is now routinely observed that while only about 4 percent of self-identifying African Americans declared themselves on the 2000 Census as having any mixture, more than 75 percent of this group are understood by demographers to be of mixed ancestry.[32] White racism, at its extreme, is manifest in the practice of hypodescent racialization, which for so long erased from public recognition this fact of widespread black-white mixing. This practice, which originated in the desire of slaveholders to classify as property the mixed-descent offspring of the children of slave women, has embodied a total rejection of one line of descent, and it has implied a uniquely severe revulsion toward that line of descent on the part of empowered whites.[33]

At stake in making empirically warranted distinctions between the various minority descent groups, and within them, is the more precise location of the barriers that inhibit Americans of various descent communities from participating more fully in American life. The more confident we can be about the social location of these barriers, the more likely is the United States to develop policies that target remedy to wrong. White racism affects its victims very differently depending on their circumstances, especially those circumstances that we call, for lack of a better word, "class." Even color is not a reliable predictor. If black immigrants from Jamaica and Africa manage to do better in this society, as measured by standard indicators, than do blacks carrying the weight of a particular history of the United States, surely this truth needs to be confronted and its possible implications for public policy honestly assessed.[34] *Postethnic America* is, among other things, an effort to encourage a more comprehensive confrontation with, and assessment of, the actual structure of inequality in American life.

This brings me to the third and last of the issues on which I want to concentrate in this "Postscript 2005," the wisdom of the system of classification employed by the U.S. Census. It was this heightened recognition of the fact of demographic mixing even within the "black" population and greater social acceptance of such mixing, that led to the epochal decision of the Census Bureau to allow respondents to mark more than one "race" in Census 2000. And it was the need for accurate measurements of ethnoracial minorities protected by antidiscrimination laws (especially the Voting Rights Act of 1965) that led the federal Office of Management and Budget to instruct the Census Bureau to "allocate" to "the minority race" those "responses that combine one minority race and white."[35] Thus the federal government quietly reinserted into the tabulation of the census the principle of hypodescent that the opportunity to mark "more than one" was publicly said to repudiate. The tension between the need of individual cultural identity and the needs of antidiscrimination measures is now vividly displayed in the gap between the actual census forms, on the one hand, and the tabulation practices of the government on the other. This is exactly the tension that led me, in "Postscript 2000" (pages 179–182), to suggest two separate questions on the census: one designed to count people according to their self-proclaimed cultural affiliations with descent groups and another designed to count people according to their perceived vulnerability to discrimination at the hands of empowered whites.

The logic of this proposal has appealed to some academic commentators, but the notion of two separate questions having to do with basic group identity has proved too complicated to generate any real pressure to put this proposal into effect in the 2010 census. I still believe this would be the best solution because it openly explains to the public the main reasons for counting at all, and it would explain further that both of the two main justifications end up thwarting each other if they are not clearly separated.[36] But a considerably more modest reform could be put into immediate effect.

The word *race* could easily be dropped from the census even while preserving the new opportunity to identify with the same ethnoracial groups that now define the "race question"— the large, so-called "panethnic" groups—and while preserving the government's practice of hypodescent allocation for antidiscrimination purposes. In one of the most cogent assessments of census issues yet contributed to the current debates, former Census Bureau chief Kenneth Prewitt has criticized his successors for not taking this possibility seriously.[37] Respondents could be asked to mark one or more of the six basic categories of the 2010 census ("Hawaiian and Pacific Islander" was added to the five groups of the ethnoracial pentagon just prior to the 2000 census as a result of lobbying led by a senator from Hawaii), but these categories could be described simply as "population groups" or "primary identity groups." They might even be described as "racial and ethnic groups." This last phrasing would be the weakest version of this reform, because it retains *race*, but even this version would at least erase the race-ethnicity distinction, eliminate the need for the anomalous treatment of Hispanics as an ethnic group that could be of "any race," do away with the even more awkward "Non-Hispanic White" category, and diminish the pressure to have Latinos classified as a "race," because in this scheme they would have the same standing in the census as the groups currently called "races" and the same protections in relation to antidiscrimination remedies.

Yet the case for classifying and counting Americans by the large, panethnic categories is not as obvious as it once was. The lines between the five color-coded groups are becoming less distinct. The internal diversity of these groups has become harder to ignore. And recent politics makes it all too clear that these categories are political artifacts: the number of such categories can be expanded by sheer force of political lobbying. Prewitt points out that Hawaiians and Pacific Islanders are not the only group that can make a credible case for a distinctive history and a record of being abused: since the whole enterprise of ethnic and racial classification has long since turned its back on science, "it is difficult to arrive at a public consensus on how many racial and ethnic groups there are in America."[38] The pentagon-plus-one leaves up for grabs whether Americans who trace their descent to India or Iran or Turkey are "Asian Americans" (usually not, in popular understanding; but does that mean they are "white"?) and speaks not at all to the Arab population whose origins span the divide between Asia and Africa. This now-six-part structure also assumes that Hispanics from Cuba, Puerto Rico, Mexico, Guatemala, and Argentina are all similar enough to be part of the same group and leaves vague the status of people whose ancestry is in Brazil or Portugal or Spain. But there is a way around this problem, one fully compatible with the collecting of data relevant to the enforcement of civil rights legislation and with the preservation of the more-than-one option.

The census might drop some or all of the large "panethnic" categories and count instead those inhabitants who identify with descent communities from specific countries or regions. Any public or private agency that wished for any reason—including the design and enforcement of antidiscrimination remedies—could combine the numbers of people who selected Mexico, Cuba, Puerto Rico, Guatemala, etc., and have a functionally "Hispanic" set of statistics. Yet such an agency would have the capacity to deselect Portuguese Americans and Spanish Americans, for example, if they chose to do so. The same applies to Americans who selected China, Japan, Korea, the Philippines, Vietnam, India, Pakistan, Iran, Syria, Egypt, Morocco, etc. Aggregation is possible, depending on the mission of the agency using the census data and the salience to that mission of the distinction between East Asians, South Asians, and Middle Eastern Asians. What about persons of African descent? There is no compelling reason not to simply list "Africa" as among the choices, since most Americans of African descent do not identify with specific countries or regions within Africa and since statistics about persons of African descent are by far the most pertinent to antidiscrimination remedies. Valuable data distinguishing recent immigrants from Africa and the Caribbean and their descendants from others with African ancestry can be gleaned from other immigration-related segments of the census. "Europe" would do well enough for what has been called "white," although a listing of European national identities subject to aggregation is also a reasonable way to measure the uniquely privileged white population of the United States. American Indians, already a category of exceedingly porous boundaries, could remain unchanged or particularized by specific tribe.

Would this reform of the basic categories of the census be fully responsive to the demographic complexities of American society? Of course not. But the complexities it ignores and the confusions it might create need to be critically assessed in comparison with those of its rivals, especially the system now in place. This more particularized system would recognize the identity claims of a great number of specific descent communities within the populations to which the panethnic terms "Asian American" and "Hispanic" are blind. It would also enable authorities to measure more accurately the progress of specific descent groups in overcoming the obstacles of white racism and economic hardship and thus to sharpen the ability of authorities to target remedy to wrong. This system would facilitate the more precise tracking of income, residence, marriage, reproduction, and other social indicators. It would be consistent, therefore, with the argument I made above for the greater recognition of differences between, and within, minority descent groups. It would give the scientific pretensions of the census more credibility because it would deal with closer-to-the-ground descent communities. This reform would also get the Census Bureau out of the de facto role of deciding in advance what groups were the victims of prejudice; a key to the special status given to Hawaiians and Pacific Islanders, after all, was the evidence of their victimization. Data collected in these more particular categories would better enable public and private agencies to determine where disadvantage lies and what causes it. Surely this would serve the cause of equality better than expecting such agencies to work with data in categories the very selection of which were made on the basis of a prior judgment as to which groups were disadvantaged.

The radical reform of the census categories for which I am arguing here can thus be defended from a public policy point of view. Since counting is incidental to classifying, as scholars have emphasized again and again, the census categories demand a clear and consistent justification. A major function of the census is simply to classify, to enact a decision made by the state concerning how people should see themselves and in relation to one another. Which distinctions between the inhabitants really matter and which do not? With whom are individuals encouraged to affiliate? Many Americans think of the census as descriptive, as something that describes for us what the society is like. Yet it is also massively prescriptive. Credit for developing this insight into the power of the state-disseminated vocabularies to influence the self-perception and affiliations of individuals is often given to the French sociologist Pierre Bourdieu, but the insight has been articulated and applied with great force in relation to the recent American census debates by many scholars, including Prewitt and Melissa Nobles.[39] The more it is understood that counting is incidental to classifying, the more important it becomes to have a clear public justification for any system of classification.[40] No such justification for the existing system has been offered by the government of the United States. An advantage of the reform I outline above is that it minimizes prescriptive identities beyond a) those most immediately functional in facilitating antidiscrimination remedies, and b) those that carry actual cultural traditions that individuals may wish to affirm. Hence the two goals that I earlier sought to advance with two separate questions—voluntary cultural affiliation and antidiscrimination enforcement—might still be achieved through a single question, if radically reformulated.

In concluding this "Postscript 2005" I want to return to one of the central concerns driving this project from its inception. This concern has become more intense for me in the decade during which I have added the two postscripts and written a number of follow-up essays now collected in another book, *Cosmopolitanism and Solidarity.*[41] The concern is that the United States will give up too easily on the challenge of critically revising its tradition of civic nationalism, and that its citizens will instead allocate more and more of their energies to the defense of economic privilege, to the flourishing of religious affiliations, and to the preservation of descent-defined communities. Fewer and fewer political leaders of the early twenty-first century advocate a strong national solidarity except in relation to the support of military action abroad. The notion that Americans are "all in it together" within the borders of the country is mocked by the decline of public education and other social services. A succession of government leaders are slow to vindicate government as a potentially enlightened instrument of the democratic public, and play instead to this or that segment of the electorate's easy retreat into smaller and more private loyalties, transcended only in the name of national defense. I concluded the first edition of this book (page 172) with the observation that even the least empowered of individuals have at least some choices about with whom to build solidarities, with whom to try to draw one's "circles of the we." That is still true, and the stakes are higher than ever.

Berkeley, California

August 2005

NOTES

CHAPTER 1: INTRODUCTION

1. Mitchell Cohen, "Rooted Cosmopolitanism," *Dissent*, Fall 1992, 487–83; Bruce Ackerman, "Rooted Cosmopolitanism," *Ethics* 104 (1994): 516–35.
2. Ernesto Laclau and Chantal Mouffe, *Hegemony and Socialist Strategy: Toward a Radical Democratic Politics* (London, 1985), 4.
3. Ernest Gellner, *Postmodernism, Reason and Religion* (New York, 1992); Arthur M. Schlesinger, Jr., *The Disuniting of America: Reflections on a Multicultural Society* (New York, 1992).
4. Robert Hughes, *The Culture of Complaint: The Fraying of America* (New York, 1993). For a discerning review of this book by a defender of multiculturalism whom I would classify as more of a cosmopolitan than a pluralist, see Henry Louis Gates, Jr., "The Weaning of America," *New Yorker*, April 19, 1993, 113–17.
5. The word *postethnic* first came to my attention when I saw

it in Werner Sollors, "A Critique of Pure Pluralism," in *The Reconstructing of American Literary History,* ed. Sacvan Bercovitch (Cambridge, Mass., 1986), 277.

6. This point about the significance of vocabulary—speaking of "affiliations" instead of "identities"—is one almost articulated, but not quite, by the Chicago Cultural Studies Group, "Critical Multiculturalism," *Critical Inquiry* 18 (1992); see esp. 541, 548.

7. A recent book that makes this complaint convincingly is Russell Jacoby, *Dogmatic Wisdom: How the Culture Wars Divert Education and Distract America* (New York, 1994).

8. See, for example, Richard Bernstein, *The Dictatorship of Virtue: Multiculturalism and the Battle for America's Future* (New York, 1994)

CHAPTER 2: HALEY'S CHOICE AND THE ETHNO-RACIAL PENTAGON

1. Ishmael Reed et al., "Is Ethnicity Obsolete?" in *The Invention of Ethnicity,* ed. Werner Sollors (New York, 1989), 227, commenting on Alex Haley, *Roots: The Saga of an American Family* (New York, 1976).

2. This list is confined to labels understood to be morally neutral or honorific, but the representation of ethnic and racial differences in American life includes the colloquial epithets that correspond to the socially accepted labels listed here.

3. Of the many writings addressed to this theme, a recent collection of essays by twenty black intellectuals is exceptionally helpful: Gerald Early, ed., *Lure and Loathing: Essays on Race, Identity, and the Ambivalence of Assimilation* (New York, 1993).

4. Reed, "Is Ethnicity Obsolete?" 229.

5. For a recent summary of this record of inequality as it

applies to African Americans, see Andrew Hacker, *Two Nations: Black and White, Separate, Hostile, Unequal* (New York, 1992).

6. In speaking of American nationality, I do not mean that virtually everyone was an egalitarian in theory and choked only when it came time to put the theory into practice. The theory itself was often contested by people who preferred more narrowly communitarian and ethno-racially homogeneous visions of nationality. Regarding efforts to move the theory of American citizenship in ethnic directions, see Rogers M. Smith, "The 'American Creed' and American Identity: The Limits of Liberal Citizenship in the United States," *Western Political Quarterly* 41 (1988): 225–51.

7. Will Herberg, *Protestant-Catholic-Jew: An Essay in American Religious Sociology* (Garden City, N.Y., 1955). Although Herberg's book popularized and developed this notion, it was introduced by Ruby Jo Reeves Kennedy, "Single or Triple Melting Pot," *American Journal of Sociology* 49 (1944): 331–39.

8. "Each course will take substantial account of groups drawn from at least three of the following: African Americans, American Indians, Asian Americans, Chicano/Latinos, and European Americans." Regulation 300, *Regulations of the Berkeley Division of the Academic Senate of the University of California*, adopted April 1989.

9. This point is made by the journalist Bob Callahan in a clever account of a decision by the California Arts Council concerning who was and was not a minority; see Callahan's contribution to the symposium, "Is Ethnicity Obsolete?" in *Invention of Ethnicity*, 232.

10. Barbara J. Fields, "Ideology and Race in American History," in *Region, Race, and Reconstruction*, ed. Morgan Kousser et al. (New York, 1982), 149.

11. *United States v. Bhagat Singh Thind*, 261 U.S. 206 (1923).

12. The work of the historian David Roediger has been especially valuable in tracing the growth in political and economic significance of the category of whiteness. See his *The Wages of Whiteness: Race and the Making of the American Working Class* (New York, 1991); and *Toward an Abolition of Whiteness: Essays on Race, Politics, and Working Class History* (New York, 1994), esp. 181–98.

13. This is reported in the course of an informative overview of controversies over the ethnic and racial categories employed by the federal government: Lawrence Wright, "One Drop of Blood," *New Yorker,* July 25, 1994, 47.

14. For an accessible review of scientific opinion, see James C. King, *The Biology of Race* (Berkeley, 1981).

15. Anthony Appiah, *In My Father's House: Africa in the Philosophy of Culture* (New York, 1992), 38. Appiah also provides an unusually cogent and helpful summary (pp. 35–36) of recent genetics in relation to the concept of race.

16. The decision: use it in quotation marks in the title of the book, and let it go without quotation marks in the text itself. See Henry Louis Gates, Jr., *"Race," Writing, and Difference* (Chicago, 1986). See especially Gates's concluding remarks, "Talkin' That Talk," 402–9.

17. For an informed and accessible discussion of the issue of the racial or ethnic status of Mexican Americans, see Peter Skerry, *The Mexican-Americans: The Ambivalent Minority* (New York, 1993), 15–18.

18. A representative example of this caution is Michael Omni and Howard Winant, *Racial Formation in the United States from the 1960s to the 1990s,* 2d ed. (New York, 1994), 14–24, and esp. 70.

19. I believe this solution meets the objections raised against the dropping of the category race by Omni and Winant, *Racial Formation,* esp. 54–55, 158–59, 181, and is consistent with their understanding of how "races" are socially constructed.

20. Mary C. Waters, *Ethnic Options: Choosing Identities in America* (Berkeley, 1990), 147. See also Richard D. Alba, *Ethnic Identity: The Transformation of White America* (New Haven, 1990).

21. Herbert Gans, "Symbolic Ethnicity in America," *Ethnic and Racial Studies* 2 (1979): 1–20, esp. 9.

22. Waters, *Ethnic Options*, 157–58, 164.

23. Ibid., 167.

24. Bureau of the Census, *Statistical Abstract of the United States*, 110th ed. (Washington, D.C., 1991), table 53; Wright, "One Drop," 49.

25. Carlos A. Fernandez, "La Raza and the Melting Pot," in *Racially Mixed People in America*, ed. Maria P. P. Root (Newbury Park, Calif., 1992), 139.

26. See, e.g., "U.S. Racial Categories Criticized by Minorities," *San Francisco Chronicle*, July 15, 1994. For a helpful history of the one-drop rule and for a discussion of the basis for its continued support within the ranks of African Americans today, see F. James Davis, *Who Is Black?* (University Park, Pa., 1991), esp. 180–81.

27. Wright, "One Drop," 54–55.

28. See Paul Spickard, *Mixed Blood: Intermarriage and Ethnic Identity in Twentieth-Century America* (Madison, Wis., 1989), and Paul Spickard, "The Illogic of American Racial Categories," in Root, *Racially Mixed People*, 12–23.

29. Terry Wilson, "Blood Quantum: Native American Mixed Bloods," in Root, *Racially Mixed People*, 121.

30. Wright, "One Drop," 53.

31. *Malone v. Haley*, Massachusetts Supreme Judicial Court, July 5, 1989.

32. Christopher A. Ford, "The Administration of Identity in Race-Conscious Law," *California Law Review* (October 1994): 1282.

33. Ibid., 1285.

34. "How Many Racial Categories Should the U.S. Census Have?" *San Francisco Chronicle*, August 22, 1994, p. B3.
35. David Harvey, "Class Relations, Social Justice, and the Politics of Difference," in *Place and the Politics of Identity*, ed. Michael Keith and Steve Pile (New York, 1993), 64.

CHAPTER 3: FROM SPECIES TO ETHNOS

1. Alfred Kinsey et al., *Sexual Behavior in the Human Male* (Philadelphia, 1948), and *Sexual Behavior in the Human Female* (Philadelphia, 1953).
2. See, for example, Lionel Trilling's review in the April 1948 issue of *Partisan Review*, reprinted in Trilling, *The Liberal Imagination: Essays on Literature and Society* (New York, 1950), esp. 222. Kinsey himself acknowledged that he and his staff had studied North Americans, and only those of certain social categories, but he retained his sweeping titles and his zoological persona.
3. Wendell L. Willkie, *One World* (New York, 1943). For a revealing study of this remarkable mix of anticolonialism, provincialism, and internationalism, and for a detailed account of its reception and of the circumstances surrounding its composition, see John M. Jordan, "A Small World of Little Americans: The $1 Diplomacy of Wendell Willkie's *One World*," *Indiana Magazine of History* 88 (1992): 173–204.
4. Edward Steichen, *The Family of Man* (New York, 1955).
5. These two books are among the great artifacts of the universalist enthusiasm of the midcentury era. Carey McWilliams, *Brothers under the Skin*, 3d ed. (Boston, 1964), was first published in 1943, then again in 1951 and yet again in 1964, with each edition registering the progress of civil rights consciousness in the United States. Joseph Campbell, *The Hero with a Thousand Faces* (Princeton,

1949), comments on human similarity and difference in his preface (viii).

6. Thomas Nagel, *The View from Nowhere* (New York, 1986).
7. Isaacs was one of the first observers to comment systematically upon this phenomenon in global perspective: see his *Idols of the Tribe: Group Identity and Political Change*, 2d ed. (Cambridge, Mass., 1989).
8. Erik Erikson, *Life History and the Historical Moment* (New York, 1975), 176–79. For Erikson's debate with Newton, see Kai E. Erikson, ed., *In Search of Common Ground: Conversations with Erik H. Erikson and Huey P. Newton* (New York, 1973), esp. 56–58, 61, and 127.
9. Jacob Bronowski, *The Ascent of Man* (Boston, 1973).
10. An account of the involuntary sterilizations carried out by American medical personnel in the 1930s, especially, can be found in Daniel J. Kevles, *In the Name of Eugenics: Genetics and the Uses of Human Heredity* (New York, 1985), esp. 115–17.
11. Michel Foucault, *Language, Counter-Memory, Practice: Selected Essays*, trans. Donald F. Bouchard and Sherry Simon (Ithaca, N.Y., 1977), 154.
12. In using the word *historicism* to denote this recognition of historicity, I follow a modern convention adopted by historians and most social scientists and humanistic scholars. Some philosophers and literary scholars still resist this usage and hold instead to the older, German idealist sense of the term as conveying a belief in an absolute meaning to history that reflects an absolute will.
13. Thomas S. Kuhn, *The Structure of Scientific Revolutions* (Chicago, 1962). I have emphasized the role of this book in consolidating a tradition of historicist thinking; see my "T. S. Kuhn's Theory of Science and Its Implications for History," *American Historical Review* 78 (1973): 370–93, and my "Free Enterprise and Free Inquiry: The Emergence of Laissez-

Faire Communitarianism in the Ideology of Science in the United States," *New Literary History* 21 (1990): 897–919.

14. Clifford Geertz, *Local Knowledge: Further Essays in Interpretive Anthropology* (New York, 1983), 16.

15. Eric R. Wolf, *Europe and the People Without History* (Berkeley, Calif., 1982), 391.

16. Perhaps the most widely discussed single manifestation of this impulse among anthropologists is James Clifford and George E. Marcus, eds., *Writing Culture: The Poetics and Politics of Ethnography* (Berkeley, Calif., 1986).

17. Renato Rosaldo, *Culture and Truth: The Remaking of Social Analysis* (Boston, 1989), esp. 1–21.

18. Sherry B. Ortner, "Ethnography Among the Newark: The Class of '58 of Weequahic High School," *Michigan Quarterly Review* 32 (1993): 411–29.

19. John Rawls, "Justice as Fairness: Political Not Metaphysical," *Philosophy and Public Affairs* 14 (1985): 223–52, and Rawls, "The Idea of an Overlapping Consensus," *Oxford Journal of Legal Studies* 7 (1987): 1–25.

20. "Ethnic," *Oxford English Dictionary*.

21. Gerald Early, "American Education and the Postmodernist Impulse," *American Quarterly* 45 (1993): 223. This is a lucid and perspicacious critique of what I would call the pluralist side of multiculturalism.

22. Stanley Fish, *Is There a Text in this Class? The Authority of Interpretive Communities* (Cambridge, Mass., 1980).

23. Michael Walzer, *Spheres of Justice: A Defense of Pluralism and Equality* (New York, 1983), xiv.

24. Richard Rorty, "On Ethnocentrism," *Michigan Quarterly Review* 25 (1986): 533. See also Clifford Geertz, "The Uses of Diversity," *Michigan Quarterly Review* 25 (1986): 105–23.

25. Geertz, *Local Knowledge,* 153.

26. Bernard Williams, "Left-Wing Wittgenstein, Right-Wing Marx," *Common Knowledge* 1 (1992): 42. See also Susan

Wolf, "Comment," in *Multiculturalism and "The Politics of Recognition," An Essay by Charles Taylor,* ed. Amy Gutmann (Princeton, 1992), 85; S. P. Mohanty, "Us and Them: On the Philosophical Bases of Political Criticism," *Yale Journal of Criticism* 2 (1989): 1–31; Zygmunt Bauman, *Legislators and Interpreters: On Modernity, Post-Modernity and Intellectuals* (Ithaca, N.Y., 1987), esp. 5; Jeffrey C. Alexander, "Bringing Democracy Back In: Universalistic Solidarity and the Civil Sphere," in *Intellectuals and Politics,* ed. Charles Lemert (London, 1991), 157–76; and Marion Smiley, *Moral Responsibility and the Boundaries of Community: Power and Accountability from a Pragmatic Point of View* (Chicago, 1992), esp. 12, 24–25.

27. Peter Novick, *That Noble Dream: The "Objectivity Question" and the American Historical Profession* (New York, 1988), 469–71; Carl Becker's famous essay was reprinted in a book of the same title, *Everyman His Own Historian* (New York, 1935), 232–55. Becker addressed both personal and tribal contexts for the exercise of the historical imagination. While Novick's phrase, "Every Group Its Own Historian," neatly catches the trend to which I refer, I want to acknowledge that this phrase risks leaving the mistaken impression that exclusivist ideologies have characterized the bulk of scholarly work in ethno-racial and gender studies during the last generation. Many scholars who identify with the subject matter of these studies have welcomed other scholars of both genders and of all ethno-racial affiliations to join in the study of "their" group.

28. Thomas S. Kuhn, "Rhetoric and Liberation," as cited by Thomas L. Haskell, "The Curious Persistence of Rights Talk in the 'Age of Interpretation,'" *Journal of American History* 74 (1987): 1011.

29. Richard Rorty, "Postmodernist Bourgeois Liberalism," *Journal of Philosophy* 80 (1983): 588.

30. Rorty, *Contingency*, 191.

31. Ibid., 192.

32. Ibid., 196, 198. See also Rorty's remarks in the introduction to his collection of 1991, *Objectivity, Relativism, and Truth* (New York, 1991), 2: there, Rorty defends "an *ethnos* which prides itself on its suspicion of ethnocentrism."

33. Richard Rorty, "Human Rights, Rationality, and Sentimentality," *Yale Review* 83 (Autumn 1993): 1–20, esp. 10, 12. Rorty draws inspiration, and some of his specific terms in this essay, from the Argentinean philosopher Eduardo Rabossi.

34. Geertz, "Uses of Diversity," 122.

35. Martha Nussbaum, "Human Functioning and Social Justice: In Defense of Aristotelian Essentialism," *Political Theory* 20 (1992): 203–4.

CHAPTER 4: PLURALISM, COSMOPOLITANISM, AND THE DIVERSIFICATION OF DIVERSITY

1. A striking example of this reinscription of polarities is Evan Carton, "The Self Besieged: American Identity on Campus and in the Gulf," *Tikkun* 6 (July/August 1991): 40–47, which characterizes as "Operation Campus Storm" criticisms of multiculturalism and attacks on political correctness published in *Time, Newsweek,* the *New Republic,* and *Atlantic*. Carton links these criticisms to Operation Desert Storm in the Persian Gulf and treats as a fair emblem for the debate George Will's praise for Lynne Cheney as the nation's "secretary of domestic defense."

2. For an example of the use of this term, ostensibly as a description of opponents of multiculturalism, see Michael Geyer, "Multiculturalism and the Politics of General Education," *Critical Inquiry* 19 (1993): esp. 513–14. This arti-

cle is refreshing in its theoretical ambitions and global range.

3. The term *Eurocentric* may be fair, however, as applied to Lewis S. Feuer, who identifies "disease and massacre" as the "principal offerings" of "Central African culture," and attacks multiculturalism as "a secession from Western Civilization" comparable to that carried out by the Christian anti-intellectual sects who burned the library in ancient Alexandria. See Feuer, "From Pluralism to Multiculturalism," *Society* 29 (1991): 19–22. For an example of a more cautious defense of a curriculum concentrating on the cultural traditions of Europe, especially on the grounds that these traditions promote tolerance and diversity, see Donald Kagan, "Western Values Are Central," *New York Times*, May 4, 1991, sec. 4, p. 15.

4. For an agitated example of this insistence, see Reed Way Dasenbrock, "The Multicultural Woot," *Dissent*, (Fall 1991): 550–55.

5. Henry Louis Gates, Jr., "Goodbye, Columbus? Notes on the Culture of Criticism," *American Literary History* 3 (1991): 711–27, esp. 725; see also Henry Louis Gates, Jr., "The Weaning of America," *New Yorker*, April 19, 1993, 113–17.

6. Diane Ravitch, "Multiculturalism," *American Scholar* 59 (1990): 337–54; and Ravitch, "In the Multiculturalist Trenches," *Contention* 1 (1992): 29–36.

7. Joseph Raz, "Liberal Multiculturalism," *Dissent* (Winter 1994): 67–79; Chicago Cultural Studies Group, Jr., "Critical Multiculturalism," *Critical Inquiry* 18 (Spring 1992): 530–55.

8. Gary B. Nash, "The Great Multicultural Debate," *Contention* 1 (1992): 11.

9. See the three books, for different grade levels, by Beverley J. Armento, Gary B. Nash, Christopher L. Salter, and Karen K. Wixson, all published by Houghton Mifflin

(Boston, 1991): *From Sea to Shining Sea, America Will Be,* and *A More Perfect Union.* These books devote extensive and sympathetic attention to a great variety of American ethno-racial groups, and interpret the major episodes in the history of British North America and the United States in terms consistent with the antiracist scholarship of professional historians during the past generation.

10. Nash, "The Great Multicultural Debate," 23–25.

11. Ibid. Nash's intervention in the multicultural debate can be compared with that of another historian, Elizabeth Fox-Genovese, "Between Individualism and Fragmentation: American Culture and the New Literary Studies of Race and Gender," *American Quarterly* 42 (1990): 7–34.

12. There exists a rich scholarly literature on this history that has been drawn upon only rarely in the public debates about multiculturalism. Among the most helpful works are the many contributions of Philip Gleason, recently collected in Philip Gleason, *Speaking of Diversity* (Baltimore, 1992). Other valuable contributions include John Higham, "Ethnic Pluralism in Modern American Thought," in Higham's *Send These to Me: Immigrants in American Life,* 2d ed. (Baltimore, 1984), 198–232; Olivier Zunz, "The Genesis of American Pluralism," *Tocqueville Review* 9 (1988): 201–19; F. H. Matthews, "The Revolt Against Americanism: Cultural Pluralism and Cultural Relativism as an Ideology of Liberation," *Canadian Review of American Studies* 1 (1970): 4–31; and Lawrence H. Fuchs, *The American Kaleidoscope: Race, Ethnicity, and the Civic Culture* (Middletown, Conn., 1990).

13. Ralph Waldo Emerson, *Journals of Ralph Waldo Emerson* (Boston, 1909–1914) 7: 115–16.

14. Herman Melville, *Redburn* (1849; reprint, Harmondsworth, England, 1976), 239.

15. The commanding work on this important aspect of the his-

tory of the United States remains John Higham, *Strangers in the Land: Patterns in American Nativism, 1860–1925* (New Brunswick, N.J., 1955).

16. Melville, *Redburn*, 238.

17. John Bryant, "'Nowhere a Stranger': Melville and Cosmopolitanism," *Nineteenth-Century Fiction* 39 (1984): 275–91. In *The Confidence-Man* (New York, 1857), Melville paid his own respects to the shifty character then taken by American nationalists to be explicitly cosmopolitan.

18. Horace Kallen, "Democracy Versus the Melting Pot," *Nation* 100 (February 18–25, 1915): 190–94, 217–20; Kallen, *Culture and Democracy in the United States* (New York, 1924).

19. Dewey's words are from his letter to Kallen, March 3, 1915, as quoted by Robert Westbrook, *John Dewey and American Democracy* (Ithaca, N.Y., 1991), 214.

20. Randolph Bourne, "Trans-National America," *Atlantic Monthly* 118 (July 1916): 86–97. This essay has been widely reprinted, including in David A. Hollinger and Charles Capper, eds., *The American Intellectual Tradition*, 2d ed., vol. 2 (New York, 1993), 179–88.

21. Wallace Stegner, *One Nation* (New York, 1945). A remarkable feature of this book, completed while the war with Japan was still in progress, is its scathing criticism of the internment of Japanese Americans.

22. See, for example, Everett R. Clinchey, *All in the Name of God* (New York, 1934), 163–79.

23. I have discussed these intellectuals and their historic role in "Ethnic Diversity, Cosmopolitanism, and the Emergence of the American Liberal Intelligentsia," *American Quarterly* 27 (1975): 133–51.

24. Herberg, *Protestant-Catholic-Jew: An Essay in American Religious Sociology* (Garden City, N.Y., 1995), 20.

25. W. E. B. Du Bois, *The Souls of Black Folk* (1903; reprint, New York, 1961), esp. 16–17.

26. An example is Robert A. Orsi, *The Madonna of 115th Street: Faith and Community in Italian Harlem, 1880–1950* (New Haven, Conn., 1985). These studies also include sharply formulated and carefully documented studies of the interaction of the various groups and of their relation to public institutions. For a splendid example, see David A. Gerber, *The Making of an American Pluralism: Buffalo, New York, 1825–60* (Urbana, Ill., 1989). Gerber and several other leaders in the study of American ethnic history have together written a very useful critical summary of the state of the art: Kathleen Conzen et al., "The Invention of Ethnicity: A Perspective from the U.S.A.," *American Journal of Ethnic History* 12 (1992): 3–42.

27. Bruce Robbins, "Othering in the Academy: Professionalism and Multiculturalism," *Social Research* 58 (1991): 354–72, esp. 358–59. See also Bruce Robbins, "Comparative Cosmopolitanism," *Social Text,* (Spring 1992): 169–86.

28. Jeremy Waldron, "Minority Cultures and the Cosmopolitan Alternative," *University of Michigan Journal of Law Reform* 25 (1992): 751–92; Cohen, "Rooted Cosmopolitanism"; Tobin Siebers, "The Ethics of Anti-Ethnocentrism," *Michigan Quarterly Review* 32 (1993): 41–70; Linda Kerber, "Diversity and the Transformation of American Studies," *American Quarterly* 41 (1989): 415–31; Ackerman, "Rooted Cosmopolitanism."

29. Examples abound in the summer 1992 *October,* "The Identity Question: A Special Issue."

30. Yi-Fu Tuan, "Cultural Pluralism and Technology," *Geographical Review* 79 (1989): 279.

31. David Simpson, "Literary Criticism, Localism, and Local Knowledge," *Raritan* 14 (1994): 88.

32. Marshall Berman, "Why Modernism Still Matters," in

Modernity and Identity, ed. Scott Lash and Jonathan Friedman (Cambridge, Mass., 1992), 33–58; Angela Davis, "Rope," *New York Times,* May 24, 1992, sec. 4, p. 11; Andrew Delbanco, "The Politics of Separatism," *Partisan Review,* (Fall 1993): 534–42; Morris Dickstein, "Correcting PC," *Partisan Review,* (Fall 1993): 542–49; Todd Gitlin, "From Universality to Difference: Notes on the Fragmentation of the Idea of the Left," *Contention* 2 (1993): 15–40; Robert Hughes, *The Culture of Complaint* (New York, 1993); Itabari Njeri, "Sushi and Grits: Ethnic Identity and Conflict in a Newly Multicultural America," in Early, *Lure and Loathing,* 13–40.

CHAPTER 5: TOWARD A POSTETHNIC PERSPECTIVE

1. Numerous explorations of the problematic character of ethno-racial identity have appeared in the 1980s and 1990s. These have been generated in a variety of disciplinary contexts, including anthropology, sociology, history, philosophy, and literary studies. Prominent examples include Eugeen E. Roosens, *Creating Ethnicity: The Process of Ethnogenesis* (Newbury Park, Calif., 1989); Michael M. J. Fischer, "Ethnicity and the Postmodern Arts of Memory," in *Writing Culture: The Poetics and Politics of Ethnography,* ed. James Clifford and George E. Marcus (Berkeley, Calif., 1986), 194–233; Anthony Appiah, "'But Would That Still Be Me?' Notes on Gender, 'Race,' Ethnicity, as Sources of 'Identity,'" *Journal of Philosophy* 87 (October 1990): 493–99; and Werner Sollors, *Beyond Ethnicity: Consent and Descent in American Culture* (New York, 1986). Sollors's work has done more to redirect American discussions of ethnic identity than any other single contribution

since the classic work of Nathan Glazer and Daniel Patrick Moynihan, *Beyond the Melting Pot* (Cambridge, Mass., 1963). See also the valuable collection, Sollors, ed., *The Invention of Ethnicity* (New York, 1989), especially Sollors's own introduction (ix–xx).

2. Angela Davis, "Rope," *New York Times*, May 24, 1992, sec. 4, p. 11.

3. Jeremy Waldron, "Minority Cultures," 778.

4. Stanley Aronowitz, "Discussion," *October,* (Summer 1992): 109.

5. David Harvey, *The Condition of Postmodernity* (Cambridge, Mass., 1989), 116–17.

6. Donna Haraway, *Simians, Cyborgs, and Women* (New York, 1991), 187, emphasis in original. Haraway's important book on primatology is *Primate Visions: Gender, Race, and Nature in the World of Modern Science* (New York, 1989).

7. The best brief account of the issues raised by feminist analysis of science is Evelyn Fox Keller, "Gender and Science: 1990," in *Great Ideas Today 1990* (Chicago, 1990), 69–93. See also Helen Longino, *Science as Social Knowledge: Values and Objectivity in Scientific Inquiry* (Princeton, 1990); Sandra Harding, "After the Neutrality Ideal: Science, Politics, and 'Strong Objectivity,'" *Social Research* 59 (1992): 567–87; and Frances E. Mascia-Lees, Patricia Sharpe, and Colleen Ballerino Cohen, "The Postmodernist Turn in Anthropology: Cautions from a Feminist Perspective," *Signs* 15 (1989): 7–33. A helpful discussion of the epistemological orientation of recent historiography of science is Jan Golinski, "The Theory of Practice and the Practice of Theory: Sociological Approaches in the History of Science," *Isis* 81 (1990): 492–505. See also Joseph Rouse, "The Politics of Postmodern Philosophy of Science," *Philosophy of Science* 58 (1991): 607–27, especially 624–25; and Timothy Lenoir, "Practice, Reason, Context: The Dia-

logue between Theory and Experiment," *Science in Context* 2 (1988): 3–22.

8. Alice Walker, *Possessing the Secret of Joy* (New York, 1992).

9. For a helpful discussion, see Myra Jehlen, "Archimedes and the Paradox of Feminist Criticism," *Signs* 6 (1981): 575–601, and, responding to Jehlen, Mohanty, "Us and Them," 28–29. See also Micaela di Leonardo, "Contingencies of Value in Feminist Anthropology," in *Gendering Knowledge*, ed. Joan E. Hartman and Ellen Messer-Davidow (Austin, Tex., 1991), 140–58; and the essays collected in Chandra Mohanty, Ann Russo, and Lourdes Torres, eds., *Third World Women and the Politics of Feminism* (Bloomington, Ind., 1991).

10. Rorty often complains that Habermas too often goes "transcendental," but Richard Bernstein and Martin Jay insist that Habermas's project, especially as recently formulated, is compatible with the historicist perspective Rorty has done so much to advance. See Richard Bernstein, *Beyond Objectivism and Relativism* (Philadelphia, 1983), esp. 183, and Martin Jay, review of *The Philosophical Discourse of Modernity*, by Jurgen Habermas, *History and Theory* 28 (1989): 94–112.

11. Selya Benhabib, *Situating the Self: Gender, Community and Postmodernism in Contemporary Ethics* (New York, 1992), 228, 230. Similarities between my own case for postethnicity and Benhabib's efforts to recover valuable elements from the collapse of universalism have been noted by Paul Fideler, "Toward a 'Curriculum of Hope,'" *Teaching the Humanities*, American Council of Learned Societies Occasional Paper no. 23 (1994): 134–36.

12. Joseph Raz, "Liberal Multiculturalism," *Dissent,* (Winter 1994): 73.

13. Michael Sandel, *Liberalism and the Limits of Justice* (New

York, 1982), 179. I want to acknowledge that Sandel makes this remark in the context of an analysis more friendly to traditional communities, and more suspicious of new ones, than is the position I take here.

14. Karl Marx, "The Eighteenth Brumaire of Louis Bona-parte," reprinted in *Basic Writings on Politics and Philosophy: Karl Marx and Friedrich Engels*, ed. Lewis Feuer (New York, 1959), 320.

15. For a vigorous argument to the effect that many traditional communities should be seen as artificial rather than authentic, see Waldron, "Minority Cultures," esp. 761–66.

16. Alan Wolfe, "Democracy versus Sociology: Boundaries and Their Political Consequences," in *Cultivating Differences: Symbolic Boundaries and the Making of Inequality*, ed. Michèle Lamont and Marcel Fournier (Chicago, 1992), 319.

17. Karen Isaksen Leonard, *Making Ethnic Choices: California's Punjabi Mexican Americans* (Philadelphia, 1992), 217. The passage Leonard quotes is from Salman Rushdie, *In Good Faith* (London, 1990), 3–4 (emphasis in original).

18. For an argument that the multiculturalist debates have actually served to perpetuate racial thought under the euphemistic language of "culture," see Walter Benn Michaels, "Race into Culture: A Critical Genealogy of Cultural Identity," *Critical Inquiry* 18 (1992): 655–85, esp. 684–85.

19. The evangelical historian George Marsden has spoken extensively on this issue. See, for example, Marsden, "Church, State, and Campus," *New York Times*, April 26, 1994, sec. 4, p. 21.

20. *Wisconsin v. Yoder.* For a discussion of this case in relation to issues in ethno-racial as well as religious communal boundaries, see Nomi Stolzenberg, "'He Drew a Circle that Shut Me Out': Assimilation, Indoctrination, and the Para-

dox of a Liberal Education," *Harvard Law Review* 106 (1993): 582–667.

21. Indeed, courts have begun to address this line of reasoning. See especially *Mozert v. Hawkins County Board of Education,* in which a Tennessee court ruled in 1987 against parents who protested that required textbooks exposed their children to ideas the parents judged damaging to the kind of community the parents wanted to maintain for their children. This case, too, is helpfully addressed by Stolzenberg, "Circle."

22. A number of thoughtful reflections on pluralism in relation to the American tradition of the separation of church and state are included in James Davison Hunter and Os Guinnes, eds., *Articles of Faith, Articles of Peace: The Religious Liberty Clauses and the American Public Philosophy* (Washington, D.C., 1990).

23. See, for example, Beverley J. Armento et al., *A More Perfect Union* (Boston, 1991).

24. One major work of canon revision that might be construed as a response to exactly these political obligations is Paul Lauter et al., *The Heath Anthology of American Literature* (New York, 1990; 2d ed., 1994). For an intelligent and provocative discussion of the first edition of this collection, more suspicious of it than I am, see Richard Ruland, "Art and a Better America," *American Literary History* 3 (1991): 336–59.

25. There is in some circles an almost pathological reluctance to attribute anything of real value to a distinctly European source. A representative example is a note by which the editors of *Public Culture* explained their decision to reprint a piece by the eighteenth-century German thinker Johann Gottfried Herder. This piece inaugurated a series on the development of the concept "public." But the editors, rather than accepting their own judgment that Herder was

an appropriate selection and taking his ideas for whatever they might be worth, apologized and ritualistically proclaimed their suspicion of things European: "We thus begin with a classical European thinker—at the risk, perhaps, of lapsing into an old-fashioned Eurocentric history of ideas." See "Genealogy," *Public Culture* 5 (1993): 347.

26. For a discussion of this episode by an educator critical of it, see Diane Ravitch, "Multiculturalism," *American Scholar* 59 (1990): 346–47.

27. Martin Bernal, *Black Athena: The Afro-Asiatic Roots of Classical Civilization,* vol. 1 of *The Fabrication of Ancient Greece, 1785–1985* (New Brunswick, 1987). See also the discussion of Bernal's work and its reception in Molly Myerowitz Levine, "The Use and Abuse of *Black Athena,*" *American Historical Review* 97 (1992): 440–60.

CHAPTER 6: THE ETHNOS, THE NATION, THE WORLD

1. This distinction is proving more useful than ever to students of nationalisms, past and present. See, for example, one of the most ambitious books yet addressed to the topic, Liah Greenfeld, *Nationalism: Five Roads to Modernity* (Cambridge, Mass., 1992), esp. 11–12. The utility of the civic-ethnic distinction is accepted by Greenfeld's most effective critic, Stanley Hoffmann, whose brilliant review should be read by anyone using the Greenfeld book or otherwise interested in the difficulties of defining and addressing "nationalism": "The Passion of Modernity," *Atlantic,* August 1993, 101–8.

2. Michael Ignatieff, *Blood and Belonging: Journeys into the New Nationalism* (New York, 1994), 6–7, 249.

3. Benedict Anderson, *Imagined Communities: Reflections on*

the Origin and Spread of Nationalism, 2d ed. (New York, 1991), 47. In his preface to the second edition of this book, Anderson complained justly that most discussants of the first edition (1983) had ignored his emphasis on the New World and continued to theorize about nationalism on the basis of the "ethnolinguistic nationalism" of Europe (xii).

4. Bernard-Henri Levy, quoted in "An Alarum for the New Europe Is Sounded from a Paris Salon," *New York Times,* December 13, 1992, sec. 4, p. 9.

5. For a compelling account of Soviet sponsorship of ethnic particularism, see Yuri Slezkine, "The USSR as a Communal Apartment, or How a Socialist State Promoted Ethnic Particularism," *Slavic Review* 53 (1994): 414–52. See also the overview of this syndrome throughout the Soviet bloc of Eastern European states provided in Katherine Verdery, "Beyond the Nation in Eastern Europe," *Social Text* 38 (Spring 1994): 12–23.

6. Thomas Nagel, *Equality and Partiality* (New York, 1991), 178; Robert B. Reich, *The World of Nations: Preparing for 21st-Century Capitalism* (New York, 1991), 301–15. Reich's perspective can be instructively contrasted to the capitalism-conquers-all vision of postnationality advanced by a champion of the international business elite, Kenichi Ohmae, in *The Borderless World: Power and Strategy in the Interlocked Economy* (New York, 1990).

7. See George Yudíce, "We Are *Not* the World," *Social Text* nos. 31–32 (1992): 202–16.

8. Michael Walzer, "What Does It Mean to Be an 'American'?" *Social Research* 57 (1990): 614. Although Walzer comments extensively on Horace Kallen's development of the idea of cultural pluralism, Walzer's own position would seem to be closer to Bourne's interactionist ideal for American ethnic groups than to Kallen's tendency to encourage in each group a greater measure of internal solidarity.

9. For an enlightening discussion of this feature of national identity in the United States, see Paul G. Romano, "American National Identity: Membership, Civic Virtue, and Postethnicity in the 'Constructed' Nation," (master's thesis, Department of Political Science, University of California at Berkeley, 1993).

10. Herman Melville, *White-Jacket or The World in a Man-of-War* (1850; reprint, New York, 1979), 153.

11. Ignatieff, *Blood and Belonging*, 13.

12. Arjun Appadurai, "Patriotism and Its Futures," *Public Culture* 5 (1993): 419–20.

13. Ibid., 419.

14. Nicholas Garnham, "The Mass Media, Cultural Identity, and the Public Sphere in the Modern World," *Public Culture* 5 (1993): 259.

15. Kevin Robins, "Global Culture," in *Modernity and Its Futures*, ed. Stuart Hall, David Held, and Tony McGrew (Oxford, 1992), 317. This entire volume is an exceptionally lucid and fair-minded introduction to the political-economic and cultural circumstances now confronted by industrial societies in an era of rapidly increasing interdependence.

16. For some thoughtful remarks on the "denationalization of the state," see Zygmunt Bauman, "Modernity and Ambivalence," in *Global Culture: Nationalism, Globalization and Modernity*, ed. Mike Featherstone (London, 1990), esp. 167. This book contains a number of suggestive essays on the topics indicated by its title.

17. David Farber, *The Age of Dreams: America in the 1960s* (New York, 1994), 66.

18. I am grateful to Kenneth Cmiel for helping me to see how the crisis of the nation-state is now proceeding in the United States.

19. Reich, *Work of Nations;* James Fallows, "How the World Works," *Atlantic,* December 1993, 61–87.

20. Appadurai, "Patriotism and Its Futures," 423–25, 427.

21. For tables displaying arriving and departing immigrants by foreign nation, see Stephen Thernstrom, ed., *The Harvard Encyclopedia of American Ethnic Groups* (Cambridge, Mass., 1980), 1036. For the Polish case, see this reference work's article by Victor Green, "Poles," 787–803, esp. 798.

22. In an otherwise valuable report on research concerning immigrants from one region in Mexico, the anthropologist Roger Rouse stresses what he mistakenly takes to be the novelty of a situation in which immigrants to the United States remain closely tied to their community of origin. See Roger Rouse, "Mexican Migration and the Social Space of Postmodernism," *Diaspora* 1 (1991): 8–23, esp. 12–13.

23. For an overview of the new immigration by a historically aware sociologist, see Herbert J. Gans, "Second-Generation Decline: Scenarios for the Economic and Ethnic Futures of the Post-1965 American Immigrants," *Ethnic and Racial Studies* 15 (1992): 173–92.

24. Skerry, *Mexican-Americans*, 7.

25. For a careful exploration of the prospects of divided sovereignty, see Thomas W. Pogge, "Cosmopolitanism and Sovereignty," *Ethics* 103 (1992): 48–75. Pogge is a strong voluntarist, engaged especially by political communities of consent that override, rather than build upon, ethno-racial ties.

26. Nancy Fraser, "Rethinking the Public Sphere: A Contribution to the Critique of Actually Existing Democracy," in *The Phantom Public Sphere*, ed. Bruce Robbins (Minneapolis, 1993), 14, 18. This essay is a probing, discerning exploration of the democratic potential of a multiplicity of publics that resist separatism and engage issues of national and global scope.

27. The "juror model" is taken up by Kenneth Cmiel, "'A Broad Fluid Language of Democracy': Discovering the American Idiom," *Journal of American History* 79 (1992): 936.

28. Sheldon Wolin, "Fugitive Democracy," *Constellations* 1 (1994): 24.

29. Kathleen Sullivan, "Rainbow Republicanism," *Yale Law Journal* 47 (1988): 1721. This is a clear and helpful discussion of the theoretical problems and opportunities presented by voluntary societies in the American constitutional order. Sullivan uses the term *normative pluralism* to describe her defense of voluntary associations in the role of unabashedly partial, difference-perpetuating, culture-creating centers in a strictly private sphere outside the state. Her ideas, however, comport very well with what I take to be a postethnic perspective on group affiliation in a postethnic nation. This is especially so in view of the caveats she enters against pluralism (p. 1723).

30. For an example of the argument that a truly historical understanding of the history of culture within the United States invalidates the very concept of America and leaves disciplinary study of American literature without a real subject, see Peter Carafiol, "Commentary: After American Literature," *American Literary History* 4 (1992): 539–49. That it is the interests of the "state," rather than of any construction of "people," that are served by American literature is the conclusion even of David R. Shumway's nonsectarian, cautious study, *Creating American Civilization: A Genealogy of American Literature as an Academic Discipline* (Minneapolis, 1994), 359.

31. Barbara Herrnstein Smith, "Cult-Lit: Hirsch, Literacy, and the 'National Culture,'" *South Atlantic Quarterly* 89 (1990): 71, 78–79, 82.

32. Michael Walzer, "Multiculturalism and Individualism," *Dissent* (Spring 1994): 186.

33. Clifford Geertz, *Local Knowledge: Further Essays in Interpretive Anthropology* (New York, 1983), 16. The phrase "a people among peoples" I take from Sydney James's mono-

graph about eighteenth-century American Quakers, *A Peo-ple Among Peoples* (Cambridge, Mass., 1963).

EPILOGUE

1. Robert Post, "Cultural Heterogeneity and the Law: Pornography, Blasphemy, and the First Amendment," *California Law Review* 76 (1988): 320.
2. Glenn Loury, "The Poverty of Reason," *Boston Review* (February/March 1994): 11.
3. Jacqueline Jones, *The Dispossessed: America's Underclass from the Civil War to the Present* (New York, 1992), 292.
4. Edwin Markham, "The Outwitted," in *Poems of Edwin Markham,* ed. Charles L. Wallis (New York, 1950), 18. Markham's "The Man With the Hoe," published in 1899, vindicated the claims of laborers against the privileged classes throughout history.
5. Henry James, *The American Scene* (1907; reprint, Blooming-ton, Ind., 1968), 86, 120, 124 (emphasis in original). My understanding of James has been influenced by Ross Pos-nock, *The Trial of Curiosity: Henry James, William James, and the Challenge of Modernity* (New York, 1991). The case of James is all the more interesting because James wrote so candidly about dimensions of the personal distaste he felt in the presence of many immigrants, especially Jews.

POSTSCRIPT 2000

This postscript has been influenced by critical discussions of *Postethnic America* in print and in private correspondence. I want especially to acknowledge the long and thoughtful letters sent me by Benedict Anderson, Lawrence Blum, Leonard Fein, James Kloppenberg, Bruce Kuklick, James Livingston, Robert

Proctor, Bruce Robbins, Jim Sleeper, Stephen Steinberg, Brook Thomas, and Alex Zwerdling. I have been sensitized to several dimensions of the issues by the published comments of Alexander Aleinikoff, Amanda Anderson, Nathan Glazer, Will Kymlicka, Denis Lecorne, Michaela de Leonardo, Michael Lind, Ian Haney Lopez, Eric Lott, Daniel Sabbagh, Nikhil Singh, Alan Velie, and Michael Werz. I want to acknowledge, also, the continued stimulation of the community of faculty colleagues at Berkeley to whom the book is dedicated. Of those Berkeley colleagues not mentioned by name in the preface, several individuals whose conversations have helped shape this postscript are Pfeng Cheah, Catherine Gallagher, Samuel Scheffler, and Gerald Vizenor. Beyond Berkeley, I have profited from discussions with Seyla Benhabib, Richard Bernstein, Nancy Fraser, and Amy Gutman.

1. Among the most accessible of the books that have contributed substantially to this transformation of the debate, listed here alphabetically, are the following: Anthony Appiah and Amy Gutman, *Color Consciousness: The Political Morality of Race* (Princeton, 1998); Pheng Cheah and Bruce Robbins, eds., *Cosmopolitics: Thinking and Feeling Beyond the Nation* (Minneapolis, 1998); Paul Gilroy, *Against Race: Imagining Political Culture Beyond the Color Line* (Cambridge, 2000); Jennifer L. Hochschild, *Facing Up to the American Dream: Race, Class, and the Soul of the Nation* (Princeton, 1995); Will Kymlicka, *Multicultural Citizenship: A Liberal Theory of Group Rights* (New York, 1995); Robert McKim and Jeff McMahan, eds., *The Morality of Nationalism* (New York, 1997); Martha Nussbaum et al., *For Love of Country: Debating the Limits of Patriotism* (Boston, 1996); Ross Posnock, *Color & Culture: Black Writers and the Making of the Modern Intellectual* (Cambridge, 1998); Samuel Scheffler, *Families, Nations, and Strangers* (Lawrence, Kans., 1995); Neil J. Smelser and

Notes

Jeffrey C. Alexander, eds., *Diversity and Its Discontents: Cultural Conflict and Common Ground in Contemporary American Society* (Princeton, 1999); Rogers Smith, *Civic Ideals: Conflicting Visions of Citizenship in U. S. History* (New Haven, 1997); Werner Sollors, *Neither Black nor White yet Both: Thematic Explorations of Interracial Literature* (New York, 1997); and Gregory Stephens, *On Racial Frontiers: The New Culture of Frederick Douglass, Ralph Ellison, and Bob Marley* (New York, 1999).

2. Sections of this postscript incorporate material from several articles I completed during the interim, especially "Authority, Solidarity, and the Political Economy of Identity: The Case of the United States," *Diacritics* 29 (1999): 116–27, and "National Culture and Communities of Descent," *Reviews in American History* 26 (March 1998): 312–28. The latter includes two elements not incorporated into this postscript to which I want to call attention here: first, it develops the concept of "the will to descend," introduced in Chapter 5 (126–128), and second, it elaborates on the argument made in Chapter 6 about "national culture" in the United States (157–61). "National Culture and Communities of Descent" has been reprinted in Smelser and Alexander, *Diversity*, 357–262, in Louis Masur, ed., *The Challenge of American History* (Baltimore, 1998), 312–328, and in *Transit Circle* 1 (1998): 47–69. In this postscript I also draw upon "National Solidarity at the End of the Twentieth Century: Reflections on the United States and Liberal Nationalism," *Journal of American History* 84 (September 1997): 559–69; "Nationalism, Cosmopolitanism, and the United States," in Noah Pickus, ed., *Immigration and Citizenship in the 21st Century* (Lanham, Md., 1998), 85–99; and "Not Universalists, Not Pluralists: The New Cosmopolitans Find Their Own Way," *Constellations* 8 (2001). In an additional article not drawn upon here, I have extended the interpretation of recent American intellectual history offered in Chapter 2 (51–77): "The Disciplines and the Identity Debates, 1970–1995," *Daedalus* (Winter 1997): 333–51. This last article was reprinted in Thomas Bender and Carl Schorske, eds., *Academic Culture in Transformation* (Princeton, 1999).

3. David A. Hollinger, "Group Preferences, Cultural Diversity, and Social Democracy: Notes Toward a Theory of Affirmative Action," *Representations,* no. 55 (Summer 1996), 31–40. This article also argued for social programs targeted at poor people of all colors. It was reprinted in Robert Post and Michael Rogin, eds., *Race and Representation* (Cambridge, 1998).

4. Part of the challenge of designing viable programs, even when only black Americans are in view, is establishing and administering fair standards for deciding exactly who should be eligible for a program's benefits. "Are we to have our Nuremberg laws in response to their Nuremberg laws?" asks Jeremy Waldron in a discerning commentary on this problem. Waldron's imaginary conversation between his ideal advocate of group preferences and his ideal opponent of group preferences is the best model I know for how this difficult debate needs to be continued. See Jeremy Waldron, "Whose Nuremberg Laws?" *London Review of Books* (March 19, 1998): 14.

5. *Regents of University of California v. Bakke,* 483 U.S. 265, 311–13 (1978).

6. K. Anthony Appiah, "The Multiculturalist Misunderstanding," *New York Review of Books* (October 9, 1997): 36. This is a lucid overview of the multiculturalist debates from a viewpoint similar to my own.

7. For a helpful account of the history of the notion of identity, see Philip Gleason, "Identifying Identity: A Semantic History," *Journal of American History* 69 (1983): 910–31.

8. Erik Erikson, *Childhood and Society* (New York, 1950).

9. "I can't let the Nazis have the last word. I can't let them tell me, 'You're a Jew, you belong in this corner, this drawer.'" Quoted by Peter Schneider, "Saving Konrad Latte," *New York Times Magazine,* February 13, 2000, 54.

10. Henry Louis Gates, Jr., "White Like Me," *New Yorker,* June 17, 1996, 66–81.

11. Of the many helpful forums in recent years on what whiteness means, an especially valuable one is the special issue of *Hungry Mind Review,* no. 45 (Spring 1998), which includes a great range of

thoughtful essays, commentaries, and reviews on the question "Whiteness: What Is It?"

12. Edward S. Shapiro, *A Time for Healing: American Jewry Since World War II* (Baltimore, 1992), 256. I have addressed the opportunities and dilemmas of Jewish identity in an increasingly postethnic white America in David A. Hollinger, "Jewish Identity, Assimilation, and Multiculturalism," in Karen Mittleman, ed., *Creating America's Jews* (Philadelphia, 1998), 52–59.

13. See Edward J. Park in *Contemporary Sociology* (July 1996): 476; and Edward S. Shapiro in *The World and I* (November 1995): 283.

14. Bruce Robbins, *Feeling Global: Internationalism in Distress* (New York, 1999), 52. Amid a probing exploration of the problems faced by the left amid global politics at the beginning of the new century, Robbins also warns (51) that "in the absence of any international adversary matching international capital on its own terms," intellectuals and professionals need to be "wary" of the pretentious claim that they themselves might "constitute such an adversary," and he urges them to consider the relative efficacy of the much-maligned nation-state, including their own.

15. See David A. Hollinger, "Postethnic Nationality and the Separatism of the Rich," *Public Historian* 19 (1997): 23–28.

16. That *Postethnic America* fails to take sufficiently into account the nativist and coercive features of American nationalism as displayed in the 1910s and 1920s is a major complaint of Gary Gerstle, "Liberty, Coercion, and the Making of Americans," *Journal of American History* 84 (1997): 524–58. I have responded to this and other complaints of Gerstle's in Hollinger, "National Solidarity." See also Gerstle's reply, "The Power of Nations," *Journal of American History* 84 (1997): 576–80. My substantive disagreements with Gerstle about history and public policy are slight, yet he is determined to cast me in the role of an opponent, and to keep me there. Gerstle's part in this exchange, especially his reply, exemplifies what I characterized in the Epilogue (169–70) as the "diverting contest to see who can be the most hard-boiled about America." We too often yield to "the game of competitive

disillusionment, and are quick to accuse one another of being too optimistic." By explicitly refusing to play this game I am fated to lose it in the eyes of those who read and write by its rules. Gerstle credits me for the "pessimism" I express in my "National Solidarity," but he catches me even there in several lapses and notes triumphantly (578–79) that my "optimism occasionally breaks through." Thus I am revealed to be the opponent for whom Gerstle is manifestly searching: someone willing "to downplay the uniqueness of past coercion suffered by African-Americans and to inflate their prospects for freedom of affiliation in a postethnic future." In my own opinion, a modicum of hope requires no apology.

17. Reynolds Farley, "Racial Issues: Recent Trends in Residential Patterns and Intermarriage," in Smelser and Alexander, *Diversity*, 85–128. See also Matthijs Kalmijn, "Trends in Black/White Intermarriage," *Social Forces* 72 (1993): 119–46.

18. E.g., David Miller, *On Nationality* (New York, 1995); Yale Tamir, *Liberal Nationalism* (Princeton, 1993); Ernest B.Haas, *Nationalism, Liberalism, and Progress* (Ithaca, 1997); and several contributors to McKim and McMahan, *Morality*.

19. Will Kymlicka, "American Multiculturalism in the International Arena," *Dissent* (Fall 1998): 73–79. Kymlicka's refreshingly scrupulous critique does not accuse me of prescribing for nations other than the United States. Kymlicka worries that the "consensus" American outlook on nationalism and multiculturalism for which he takes *Postethnic America* to be "the most sophisticated defense" (74) is having disproportionate and negative influence on debates in Europe and Canada.

20. Kymlicka, "Multiculturalism," 74–75, 79.

21. Kymlicka, "Multiculturalism," 77.

22. Kymlicka comes close to recognizing this dilemma when he questions (78) that the United States, Canada, and Spain have any stronger claim to nationhood on liberal principles than do Catalonia, Puerto Rico, and Quebec. The latter three entities are just as postethnic, just as liberal, as the first three. Whatever the truth in this claim, the posing of the question effectively transfers the location of

the problem Kymlicka is addressing from the realm of "national mi-norities" (on the destiny of which a postethnic perspective is ostensi-bly pernicious) to that of civic nations or proto-nations with immigrant populations (where a postethnic perspective is ostensibly sound). Hence Kymlicka's case for group rights for national minori-ties as a matter of general liberal theory proves to be, here, largely a defense of Quebec as an exception to the pattern of illiberal traits that render minority nationalism problematic for liberals. Kymlicka tries to neutralize liberal suspicion of the nationalism of national minorities by presenting this nationalism as an example of liberal nationalism, not of illiberal nationalism.

23. Although Kymlicka's approach to multiculturalism and nationalism offers little to the study of the United States, he is right to complain that *Postethnic America* has almost nothing to say about the groups he calls national minorities within the United States: Puerto Rico, Guam, and the Indian tribes. He is also right to suppose (77) that I neglected these cases because "they are relatively peripheral, both geographically and numerically, in the American context." He is right, further, to fear that a failure of Americans to recognize these anomalous cases within the United States might lead to a failure to appreciate that other civic nations, such as Canada, confront chal-lenges more akin to dealing with the limited sovereignty of Indian tribes than to dealing with immigrant groups. For a helpful, in-formed discussion of the American Indian case in relation to the postethnic perspective, see Alan Velie, "Ethnicity, Indian Identity, and Indian Literature," *American Indian Culture and Research Jour-nal* (1999): 191–205.

24. See, e.g., Kwame Anthony Appiah, "Cosmopolitan Patriots," *Critical Inquiry* 23 (Spring 1997): 617–39.

25. For three very different, widely discussed examples of this scholar-ship, see Matthew Frye Jacobson, *Whiteness of a Different Color: European Immigrants and the Alchemy of Race* (Cambridge, 1998); David Roediger, *The Wages of Whiteness: Race and the Making of the American Working Class* (New York, 1991); and Smith, *Civic Ideals.*

Notes

Many of the colleagues and friends acknowledged in the Preface (xi–xii) and in "Postscript 2000" (267–268) have continued to help me absorb and engage the fast-moving, multiple discourses in which *Postethnic America* is entangled. Here, I want to acknowledge that "Postscript 2005" has also been influenced by conversations in Berkeley with John Lie, Robert Reich, Richard Candida Smith, and Justin Suran, and, beyond Berkeley, with David Brion Davis, Jennifer Hochschild, Joseph Magnet, Bhikhu Parekh, Kenneth Prewitt, John Skrentny, and Eric Sundquist.

1. In pursuing these issues I will be emphasizing the policy implications of *Postethnic America*, thereby responding, if only briefly, to a common criticism of this book: that it "remains," in the words of one of my most discerning critics, "well above the messy realms of policy formation or implementation." See Peter Schuck, *Diversity in America: Keeping Government at a Safe Distance* (Cambridge, Mass., 2003), 106.

2. Kwame Anthony Appiah, *The Ethics of Identity* (Princeton, 2005); Seyla Benhabib, *The Claims of Culture: Equality and Diversity in the Global Era* (Princeton, 2002); Rogers Brubaker, *Ethnicity Without Groups* (Cambridge, Mass., 2004); Amy Gutmann, *Identity and Democracy* (Princeton, 2003); John Lie, *Modern Peoplehood* (Cambridge, Mass., 2004); Rogers M. Smith, *Stories of Peoplehood: The Politics and Morals of Political Membership* (New York, 2003). Smith offers (esp. 199–204) a fair-minded commentary on what *Postethnic America* has to say about the value of a strong national solidarity and correctly flags a disagreement: I do favor a stronger sense of peoplehood on the part of the American national community than Smith does. I continue to believe that this sense of our all being "in it together" is a predicate for better tax-supported public services and for the more equitable distribution of power. My own position is closer

to that of Jeffrey Stout, as developed in his *Democracy and Tradition* (Princeton, 2004).

3. Richard T. Ford, *Racial Culture: A Critique* (Princeton, 2004).

4. Two collections that effectively represent the range and depth of this movement are Steven Vertovec and Robin Cohen, eds., *Conceiving Cosmopolitanism: Theory, Context, and Practice* (Oxford, 2002); Daniele Archibugi, ed., *Debating Cosmopolitics* (London, 2003).

5. See especially Anatol Lieven, *America Right or Wrong: An Anatomy of American Nationalism* (New York, 2004).

6. David A. Hollinger, "Postethnic America," *Contention* II (1992), 79–96.

7. A convenient example is one of the most thoughtful defenses of the wisdom of counting all Latino/Hispanic persons as members of a single group: Silvio Torres-Saillant, "Inventing the Race: Latinos and the Ethnoracial Pentagon," *Latino Studies* I (2003), 123–151.

8. See, for example, Frederick Luis Aldema, *Postethnic Narrative Criticism* (Austin, 2003) and Joel Kotkin, "Toward a Post-Ethnic Economy," in Tamar Jacoby, ed., *Reinventing the Melting Pot: The New Immigrants and What It Means To Be American* (New York, 2004), 183–197.

9. The connection between the post-black conversation and *Postethnic America* is addressed by art critic Holland Cotter, "Beyond Multiculturalism: Freedom?" *New York Times*, July 29, 2001.

10. An efficient summary of recent scholarly analyses of ethnoracial mixing as reported in federal census data and other privately commissioned studies is Jennifer D. Lee and Frank D. Dean, "America's Changing Color Lines: Immigration, Race/Ethnicity, and Multiracial Identification," *Annual Review of Sociology* XXX (2004), 221–242.

11. Lawrence Mishel, Jared Bernstein, and Sylvia Allegretto, *The State of Working America* (Ithaca, 2005).

12. One of many recent reports of increasing economic stratification is "Poverty in U.S. Grew in 2004, While Income Failed to Rise for 5th Straight Year," *New York Times* on August 31, 2005. For one of many recent reports of increasing ethnoracial mixing, see *Table MS–3: Interracial Married Couples, 1980–2002*, released by the U.S. Bureau of the Census, September 15, 2004.

13. Nor is mixture a substitute for politics. I am occasionally accused of having promoted this remarkably wrong-headed view of the dynamics of inequality in American life. I do not believe that anything I have written carries this implication, but if it does I am glad to take this opportunity to correct myself. The greater acceptance of descent mixture in our own time is obviously the result, in large part, of the political struggle that has diminished racism in the United States. It is not an event that can be understood apart from that struggle, which is far from over.

14. This is a convenient place to correct the mistaken impression that in the vision of American history set forth in *Postethnic America*, "group divisions are expected to evaporate over time." This is the characterization offered by Desmond King in his *The Liberty of Strangers: Making the American Nation* (New York, 2005), 170. I argue not against groups, but against policies and practices that discourage people from exercising what choices are within their reach in the perpetuation and formation of groups organized around common descent or indeed around any other commonality that facilitates solidarity. The point of "affiliation by revocable consent" is not, after all, that there shall be no affiliations smaller than the national community, nor that descent shall be ruled out as a basis for socially productive solidarities, but that the United States should encourage multiple affiliations that reflect the will of individuals.

15. An excellent anthology of theoretical writings, all too rarely incorporated into policy discourse about "race" in the United States and underutilized even by scholars, is Bernard Boxil, ed., *Race and Racism* (New York, 2001).

16. An especially lucid argument distinguishing this new genetic engagement from less scientifically defensible inquiries is Jerry A. Coyne, "Legends of Linnaeus," *Times Literary Supplement* (February 25, 2005), 3–4. Coyne makes the case for the continued utility of the concept of race while criticizing as deeply unsound a book that appears, at first glance, to vindicate the concept, Vincent Sarich and Frank Miele, *Race: The Reality of Human Differences* (New York, 2004).

17. A good place to follow this debate is in the pages of the *American Journal of Public Health*, where a number of scientists have set forth the pros and cons of the concept of race for the purposes of research and medical treatment. See especially the issues of September 1998 (1297–1298, 1303–1307), May 1999 (782–785), and November 2000 (1699–1702). I thank Justin Suran for calling these exchanges to my attention. See also the arguments displayed in *Daedalus*, Winter 2002 (81–94), Spring 2002 (144–146), and Winter 2005 (102–116).

18. "The concept of race as used by the Census Bureau reflects self-identification; it does not denote any clear-cut scientific definition of biological stock. The data for race represent self-classification by people according to the race with which they most closely identify. Furthermore, it is recognized that the categories of the race item include both racial and national origin or sociocultural groups." U.S. Census Bureau, B–30, released 1992.

19. Lawrence Blum, *"I'm Not a Racist, But. . . ": The Moral Quandary of Race* (Ithaca, 2002). Much of this book's value cannot be encapsulated in an easily summarized argument. In his text and his probing endnotes, Blum provides a thorough and judicious overview of the entire terrain of the theory and practice of "race and racialization," more current than the long-standard Michael Omi and Howard Winant, *Racial Formation in the United States* (New York, 2nd ed., 1994).

20. Blum, *Not a Racist*, 151.

21. David A. Hollinger, "How Wide the Circle of the We: American Intellectuals and the Problem of the Ethnos Since World War II," *American Historical Review* (April 1993), 317–337; David Theo Goldberg, *Racist Culture: Philosophy and the Politics of Meaning* (London, 1993), 75.

22. As accessed August 18, 2005.

23. John D. Skrentny, *The Minority Rights Revolution* (Cambridge, Mass., 2002) and Hugh Davis Graham, *Collision Course* (New York, 2002).

24. Advisory Board to the President's Initiative on Race, *One America in the 21st Century: Forging a New Future* (Washington D.C., 1998).

25. For an examination of this report, including documentation of the report's systematic suppression of the differences between African American experience and Asian American experience, see David A. Hollinger, "The One Drop Rule and the One Hate Rule," *Daedalus* (Winter 2005), 18–28, especially 24–25. Several paragraphs of "Postscript 2005" are drawn from this essay.

26. I want to take this opportunity to underscore a basic point about inequality and choice. *Postethnic America* does not imply that social power is equally distributed among the various descent communities or that opportunities for choice are equally available to everyone. My concept of "Haley's Choice" was designed to flag from the start—and to protest against—the radically different degrees of choice over affiliation that Americans of different groups and different circumstances actually enjoy. I distinguish sharply between the many middle-class Americans of European descent who have considerable choice in their affiliations and the non-European ethnoracial minorities who do not. Yet I do encounter readings of this book, especially on the part of students, that ascribe to me a failure to understand that power is unevenly distributed and ascribe to me, further, the naïve belief that anyone can just affiliate with any group they want to, as if their range of choices were not limited by the historical and social conditions for which the concept of "Haley's Choice" is an emblem. In a typical version of this reading, two American Studies scholars complain that "the postethnic school" (in which these scholars locate me along with Francis Fukuyama, Shelby Steele, and Arthur M. Schlesinger, Jr.) fails to understand that "social stratifications do not go away by acts of individual choice." See Armritjit Singh and Peter Schmidt, eds., *Postcolonial Theory and the United States: Race, Ethnicity, and Literature* (Jackson, Miss., 2000), 6, 44. Someone who *really* disagreed with me would argue that individual choices about affiliation are properly restricted in the interests of an individual's own community of descent. That may be the implication of George J. Sanchez, "Creating the Multicultural Nation," in John Carlos Rowe, ed., *Post-Nationalist American Studies* (Berkeley, 2000), 53–55, who thinks the cosmopolitanism of *Postethnic America* "ridiculous" for anyone worried that their own culture may be "at risk."

27. For an accessible and up-to-date overview of this remarkable case of identity transformation, see Jack Hitt, "The Newest Indians," *New York Times Magazine*, August 21, 2005, 36–41.

28. Philip Roth, *The Human Stain* (New York, 2000); Richard Powers, *The Time of Our Singing* (New York, 2003).

29. Prominent examples include Randall Kennedy, *Interracial Intimacies: Sex, Marriage, Identity and Adoption* (New York, 2003); Rachel Moran, *Interracial Intimacy: The Regulation of Race and Romance* (Chicago, 2003); Renee C. Romano, *Race Mixing: Black-White Marriage in Postwar America* (Cambridge, Mass., 2003); Stephan Talty, *Mulatto America: At the Crossroads of Black and White Culture* (New York, 2003); and Leon E. Wynter, *American Skin: Pop Culture, Big Business & The End of White America* (New York, 2002).

30. *Table MS–3, Interracial Married Couples: 1980 to 2002*, released by the U.S. Census Bureau, September 15, 2004.

31. *Census 2000 PHC-T–19, Hispanic Origin and Race of Couple House-holds, 2000, Table 1: Hispanic Origin and Race of Wife and Husband in Married-Couple Households, 2000*, and *Table 2: Opposite-Sex Unmar-ried-Partner Households, 2000*, released March 13, 2003. See also Joel Perlmann and Mary C. Waters, "Intermarriage Then and Now: Race, Generation, and the Changing Meaning of Marriage," in Nancy Foner and George Fredrickson, eds., *Not Just Black and White: His-torical and Contemporary Perspectives on Immigration, Race, and Eth-nicity in the United States* (New York, 2004), 262–277.

32. For example, Lee and Bean, "Changing Color Lines," 233.

33. For a more extensive discussion of the historic role of the "one drop rule," see David A. Hollinger, "Amalgamation and Hypodescent: The Question of Ethnoracial Mixture in the History of the United States," *American Historical Review* (December 2003), 1363–1390.

34. The prominence of Senator Barack Obama of Illinois, son of a black immigrant from Kenya, has called attention to this demographic phenomenon.

35. *Guidance on Aggregation and Allocation of Data on Race for Use in Civil Rights Monitoring and Enforcement*, issued by the Office of Management and Budget, 2000, as cited by Joel Perlmann and Mary

C. Waters, eds., *The New Race Question: How the Census Counts Multiracial Individuals* (New York, 2003), 15.

36. Jennifer Hochschild supports this two-question approach; see Hochschild, "Multiracial Identifiers in the 2000 Census, And Then What?" in Perlmann and Waters, *The New Race Question*, 360. Another sympathizer is Werner Sollors, who, after acknowledging the difficulty of formulating questions along the lines I propose, concludes as follows: "To the fact finders of the nation such questions may seem too complicated for actual use and a mere nuisance that makes their mission difficult. But will it be better to go on pretending that the census practice of data collection was just fine? Will future historians have any reason to look at "our" racial categories in Census 2000 more generously than present day historians view the Three-Fifths Compromise in the eighteenth-century factional counting of slaves?" See Sollors, "What Race are You?" in Perlmann and Waters, *The New Race Question*, 266.

37. Kenneth Prewitt, "Racial Classification in America: Where Do We Go From Here?" *Daedalus* (Winter 2005), especially 15–16. This essay of Prewitt's is an exceptionally cogent map of the current census debates and a patient, fair-minded critique of current census policies and practices.

38. Prewitt, "Racial Classification," 10.

39. Pierre Bourdieu, *Language and Symbolic Power* (Cambridge, Mass., 1991); Kenneth Prewitt, "The Census Counts, the Census Classifies," in Foner and Fredrickson, *Not Just Black and White*, 145–164; Melissa Nobles, *Shades of Citizenship: Race and the Census in Modern Politics* (Stanford, 2000).

40. The need for open political debate on census policy is emphasized in Peter Skerry, *Counting on the Census: Race, Group Identity, and the Evasion of Politics* (Washington, 2000).

41. David A. Hollinger, *Cosmopolitanism and Solidarity: Studies in Ethnoracial, Religious and Professional Affiliation in the United States* (Madison, Wisc., 2006).